ONE HUNDRED
AND ONE THINGS
Malay

ONE HUNDRED AND ONE THINGS

Malay

GHULAM-SARWAR YOUSOF

Design by Fiona Wong

PARTRIDGE

A Penguin Random House Company

ISBN: Softcover   978-1-4828-5535-7
               eBook   978-1-4828-5534-0

To order additional copies of this book, contact
Toll Free 800 101 2657 (Singapore)
Toll Free 1 800 81 7340 (Malaysia)
orders.singapore@partridgepublishing.com

www.partridgepublishing.com/singapore

Preface

This little volume is not intended to be in any way academic. Its reader, it is envisaged, will be the average person, a non-expert or one totally unfamiliar with the subject, a Malaysian or a foreigner who wishes to understand and appreciate the Malay people of Peninsular Malaysia, their culture and their mind through some of the key indicators of their identity.

This definition is based upon language as the principal identifier of community—in this case Bahasa Melayu—as a native spoken language. The only people who have traditionally used Bahasa Melayu in this precise manner are the "Melayu" people whose origins have been variously traced: people who, like many other communities, are today encountered in many different parts of the world.

In selecting the actual terminology for definition and deliberation, care has been taken to keep discussions brief, to eschew technical jargon, as well as to avoid repetition or overlap. It is hoped that this little work, by no means "complete", will be of use to some, at least, in particular those possibly approaching traditional Malay culture for the first time.

Ghulam-Sarwar Yousof

December 2015

Notes and Acknowledgements

The initial idea for this work came from a book entitled *One Hundred Things Japanese* published by Tuttle. The original intention of the present author was to restrict the entries to 100. But that proved impossible without too much of a sacrifice. Even as it stands, there may be some unnecessary entries, some omissions and what not, which, it is hoped, will be remedied in a subsequent edition. Comments from readers will be most welcome and highly appreciated.

I wish to place on record the considerable assistance rendered by several individuals. My appreciation towards making this work possible to Yau Sim Mei and Siti Nuraishah Ahmad for their observations on the contents, to Salmyyah Raheem for proofreading and to Fiona Wong for the sketches and design of the volume.

*This work is dedicated to all who understand
or do not understand the Malays as well as
to those who wish to know them better.*

A

Adat

The term *adat* refers to customary practices and traditions among Muslim communities in many different societies the world over that do not come from Islam but are derived from local cultures. It applies in a broad range of activities, including customary laws, as well as unwritten codes regulating social, political, economic and other activities.

Two kinds of *adat* laws were developed amongst the Indonesians and Malays before the 15th century. The first is *Adat Perpateh*, a matrilineal kinship structure among the Minangkabau people in Sumatra, from where it was taken to Negeri Sembilan with the migration of Minangkabau people to that state. The second was *Adat Temenggong*. Both these indigenous systems were later influenced and, to some extent, modified by Islamic and European legal systems. Negeri Sembilan is the only Malaysian state where *adat* laws actually apply, parallel to Islamic *syariah* laws, in matters related to the family.

Akad Nikah

Akad nikah or *ijab qabul*, from Arabic, is the core religious ceremony in a Muslim wedding and the only compulsory (*wajib*) one. This ceremony can be conducted by the father or a male guardian (*wali*) of the bride-to-be. In Malaysia, it is generally conducted in each state by an official (*kathi*) appointed by the state Islamic affairs department. Only family members and close friends of both families attend the *akad nikah*; it is thus a private ceremony.

Alam

The word *alam*, from Arabic, means world or universe in two distinct senses. Firstly, it refers to the earth: not the physical entity for which the more appropriate word is *dunia*, but the world as realm, inhabited by Man (*alam manusia*). Parallel to this is the idea of the invisible world (*alam ghaib*) which may be conceived of as having within it several diverse realms such as the world of spirits (*alam arwah*), the world of jin (*alam jinn*), the intermediary world or in the Christian sense purgatory (*alam barzakh*), the realm of the angels (*alam malakut*) and the world of ideas (*alam al-mithal*) in the Platonic sense and yet others.

The word *alam* also appears in combination with other words to give it certain distinctive meanings. *Alam semesta* suggests the whole created universe; *empat penjuru alam* refers to the four corners of the world. Names of Muslim rulers all over the world, including Malaysia, contain such designations as *Raja Alam* or *Shah Alam* (king of the world or lord of the universe), *mahkota alam* (crown of the world); and *dzil Allah fil alam* (God's shadow on earth).

Amuk

Amuk, better known in its old spelling, *amok*, is a wild and uncontrolled attack by a warrior or individual as a last stand when facing a crisis. In traditional Malay society, this act had a deep meaning and significance. *Amuk* was carried out by an individual or a group with the use of weapons such as the *keris*, long knife (*parang*) and axes, as well as spears. The act of *amuk* was intended to shake the enemy, to express inner frustration, as a means of self-protection or as a result of extreme shame or disgrace. It was a means of maintaining one's self-respect (*maruah*), or that of family or community. At the same, time, however, there was a clear contradiction given the values of the Malays, who, in general are said not to express their anger openly, preferring to keep the pressures within. Thus, it is when inner tension becomes unbearable that an act of *amuk* is likely to occur. Traditional Malay literature has many well-known examples of *amuk*, and cases of *amuk* do happen in modern times with the same underlying causes.

Ancak

An *ancak* is a tray made from bamboo and leaves, usually about 90 cm square and decorated with woven coconut leaves, containing various offerings to spirits during theatre performances or for other rituals, or to trap the spirits. An *ancak* is usually hung from a tree by means of four strings or, in the case of theatre performances, it is hung from the roof or on pillars on the sides of the temporary theatre (*panggung*). Upon completion of the rituals or theatre performances, the various *ancak* with the offerings intact, are placed in locations some distance away from human habitations for the consumption of spirits. Ceremonies involving such offerings are known as *buang ancak*.

Angin

Angin (the wind) is considered by the Malays as the causal agent of many diseases, including rheumatism (*sakit angin*), syphilis (*sakit angin tofan*) or possession by malicious spirits (*sakit anginmambang*). *Angin* is the most important of the four elements (*anasir*) of which every living entity is composed. Thus, any imbalance of the wind in particular and the elements in the body in general cause illnesses. There is a third, more complicated, application of the word *angin*: in this case meaning a strong desire for or obsession with something, such as a regular activity a person particularly enjoys. In theory then, one could have *angin* or passion for anything at all such as sex or sepak raga. More particularly, performing artists may have *angin* for the joget dance, mak yong or the traditional martial art (*silat*). When unable to become involved in any such performance for whatever reason such as physical illness, old age or even the lack of opportunity, artists may suffer from emotional or psychological illnesses, loss of self-worth or severe depression. Relief is then sought through direct or indirect involvement in appropriate performances. Where a "patient" is no longer able to be directly involved in a performance, he or she has merely to be present in the theatre during a performance to benefit from it. In extreme cases, elaborate ritual (*berjamu*) performances are held to achieve cure.

Angin in a healing performance in Kelantan, Malaysia.
(Photo by Ghulam-Sarwar Yousof)

Anugerah

The term *anugerah*, from Sanskrit *nugeraha* or *anugeraha*, refers to bounty or an invaluable gift given as a special favour by God. It may take the form of a long life, health, safety and wellbeing, good progeny, noble status or high standing in society.

In the context of Malaysian society and culture, *anugerah* or *kurnia* refers to a valuable gift or award given by the Yang diPertuan Agung or king of Malaysia, a Sultan, Raja or Head of State, the government or by established public institutions in return for loyalty, contribution made to the community or the nation, the proper carrying out of duties or for charitable work. Alternatively, the award or gift may be given in recognition of some outstanding ability, special talent or personal achievement by an individual or group at the state or national level.

Awards take many forms, including titles, medals, cash payments and gifts of land. Among some of the better known are *Anugerah Sastera Negara* (National Literary Award) for literature and *Anugerah Seniman Negara* (National Cultural Award) for achievements in the visual and performing arts, both awarded since 1971 after the National Cultural Congress.

The best-known forms of *anugerah* in Malaysia are the annual awards in the form of titles such as Tun, Tan Sri and Datuk awarded to outstanding individuals by the Yang diPertuan Agung as well as by Sultans and Governors of the various States on the occasion of their official birthdays.

Anyaman

Anyaman is the art of weaving screwpine (*mengkuang*), pandanus (*pandan*) leaves or other materials to create items of utility as well as of decorative value. *Anyaman* has flourished for generations at various levels of sophistication and in varying degrees of intricacy throughout the Malay Peninsula. Among the most important items resulting from this art or craft are mats (*tikar*) and food covers (*tudung saji*). Others include fans, baskets, pouches or purses and hats.

With the art being more active in villages along the east coast of the Peninsula, particularly in Terengganu, mat-weaving (*anyaman tikar*), as done by Malay women in that state, is known both for fineness of plaiting as well as variety of patterns. Apart from covering the floor, mats are used to sit or sleep upon, as well as for purpose of praying.

Mats woven from *pandan* are regarded as of superior quality, for the leaves are softer and more easily shaped. Such mats, however, are not very durable. For this reason, those woven from *mengkuang* are more popular in daily use. The process of mat weaving, which goes through several phases, requires diligence, concentration as well as expertise in the creation of patterns (*ragi* or *kelarai*) in the design (*corak*).

Anyaman or weaving. (Photo by Fiona Wong)

Asyik

Asyik is a graceful dance believed to have originated in the Patani court in the 17th century. The word *asyik*, from Arabic and Persian, means intoxicated. The dance was performed on special occasions and celebrations such as a sultan's birthday and royal weddings. It moved from Patani to Kelantan at some unknown date. By the third quarter of the 20th century, however, *asyik* had lost its court patronage, so the dance is rarely performed in its original form. The accompanying music ensemble consists of a spiked fiddle (*rebab*), inverted gongs (*canang*), hanging knobbed-gongs (*tetawak*), a pair of drums (*gondang*), two or more smaller drums known as *gendang asyik*, and at times a wooden xylophone (*gambang*).

The dance begins with the female dancers entering the performance area, seating themselves and executing the salutation (*sembah*) gesture. Through stylized movements and gestures, they then tell the story of a long-lost pet bird that once belonged to a princess. The dance ends with the dancers seated and once again doing the *sembah*.

Tarian asyik dancer. (Sketch by Fiona Wong)

Awang Batil

Awang batil is a form of solo theatre active in Perlis and on Langkawi Island in Kedah. Performances take place with a metal bowl (*batil*) player seated cross-legged on a stage or platform, without any set or scenery, and telling stories in rhythmic prose mixed with verse. The *batil* is placed on the player's lap and struck by the hand in a rhythmic manner to accompany the narration or chanting. In addition a double-reed oboe (*serunai*) may be used to provide a court setting or environment during the narration.

Awang batil stories, preserved in the oral tradition, are mostly folk tales or legends. In performances, these are embellished with dialogue, chanting or recitation and very limited acting. Costume and mask changes, which take place with those of characters, are accompanied by appropriate mime and changes in voice as well as vocal techniques.

Traditionally, *awang batil* performers used four wooden masks representing a court official (*temenggung*), a minister (*menteri* or *wadit*), a warrior (*hulubalang*) and an astrologer (*Ahli nujum*). This final mask, when used in combination with a cap, represents a tok imam or Muslim religious official. A short dagger (*keris*) is used in ceremonial situations. No costume changes are involved.

A performance begins with theatre opening (*buka panggung*) rituals, and may last from a few minutes to a couple of hours.

Awang batil performer. (Photo by Ghulam-Sarwar Yousof)

Azimat

Derived from Arabic, sometimes also pronounced in Malay as *jimat*, an *azimat* is an amulet used principally as a means of protecting oneself. Certain *azimat* are said to cause someone to fall in love with the user or to cause jealousy, while yet others are used for the maintenance of one's health. Generally, the term *azimat* implies the use of such amulets for good purposes rather than to cause harm.

An *azimat* is usually prepared by someone well versed in the Islamic religion or by a traditional medicine-man (*bomoh*). It usually takes the form of writing or a diagram drawn on paper, leaf or animal skin. The text may consist of phrases from the Holy Quran or letters of the Arabic/ Jawi alphabet. Simple diagrams or symbols may also be used either independently or in combination with letters of the alphabet. An *azimat* is either worn around the neck in a tiny silver holder or kept in some place close to one's body such as in a purse.

Azimat in Arabic script. (Sketch by Ghulam-Sarwar Yousof)

B

Badi

Badi, a word derived from Parsi and also known in north Indian languages with a slightly different meaning, refers, among Malays, to ghostly influences or vapours likely to be encountered in a location, particularly in a jungle, where hunting or slaughter of animals or wild fowl has taken place. Deer and jungle-fowl are believed to be the private property of forest elves (*orang bunian*). It is believed, for instance, that when a deer is slain, it emits, in its death-struggle, a vapour (*asap*) that remains about the spot, afflicting anyone who approaches it with disease. This vapour is *badi*; it has to be dissipated by certain rituals before the hunter can safely secure his game. The act of removing *badi* is known as *buang badi*.

Bagih

Bagih, also spelt *bagis*, is one of several traditional healing arts active in Kelantan. It involves two principal performers: a shaman (*tok bagih*) and an interrogator or interpreter (*tok minduk*). The *tok bagih* may be a male or female, while the tok minduk is usually a male. The ritual takes place in temporary theatre (*panggung*) or in a patient's house.

Following a theatre opening (*buka panggung*) ceremony in which various spirits are invoked with appropriate incantations (*mantera*), and offerings given, the patient, now brought onto the stage, either lies down on a mat or sits with outstretched legs. The *tok bagih*, seated before him, enters into a state of trance, indicated by a violent shaking of his head, torso and arms. With a bundle of areca (*pinang*) leaves in his hands, the *tok bagih* approaches the patient, and gently brushes the patient's body with the leaves for several minutes before returning to the *tok minduk*. Here, through a question and answer session, the identity of the offending spirit is established. With that, *tok bagih* brushes the patient's body several times as before until the disease-causing spirit is driven away. In some instances, the *tok bagih* massages the patient, or sucks out malicious elements from the patient through his head.

In addition to healing, a *tok bagih* may predict fortunes, bring about a recovery of lost objects, cure mental instability in women following childbirth or heal patients affected by the use of black magic. This form of traditional healing is now almost extinct in Malaysia.

Bagih performer.
(Photo by Ghulam-
Sarwar Yousof)

Bahasa Melayu

The Malay language, *Bahasa Melayu*, is regarded as one of the Austronesian languages, belonging to the Malayic family. It developed in Borneo more than 2000 years ago and spread to Sumatra, the Malay Peninsula and elsewhere. In its earliest phase, it was written in the Indian Pallava script. Early influences from Sanskrit and other Indian languages are particularly notable to this day in its vocabulary as used specific situations such as in rituals and ceremonies. These go back to the times of the Indian-influenced kingdoms such as Bujang Valley.

The language grew rapidly during the Melaka Sultanate (1401-1511). Melaka was a highly cosmopolitan city from its very beginnings, with foreigners, particularly from the Indonesian diaspora as well as the Indian sub-continent, not only founding the city and having close connections with its ruling family, but also playing important roles in its socio-cultural life. With the arrival of the Dutch and the Portuguese as conquerors, traders and residents, the European element was introduced, strengthening those from Sumatra, India, China and the Middle East.

Such developments also took place in other parts of the peninsula in the following centuries with the inflow of peoples from the north as far as Champa and from various parts of Indonesia, including the Bugis from Sulawasi, the Mandailing from Sumatra, the Javanese, the Acehnese, Boyanese and Madurese and so on. Additional noteworthy elements in Malay vocabulary may be seen from Tamil, Gujerati, Parsi, Arabic and Chinese languages, with renewed European contributions to the language becoming more significant, particularly in the development of modern *Bahasa Melayu*.

Bahasa Melayu is Malaysia's national and official language, the language of administration and education, as well as the most important means of wider communication. Existing in several different dialects as well as in standard form, it is used by members of all ethnic groups in the country. The language generally gets written in the Roman script, while in certain parts of the country, the Jawi script, based on Arabic, is used alongside the Roman script. Efforts have been made in recent decades to standardize modern Malay and its Indonesian variant, known as Bahasa Indonesia, through adjustments to the spelling systems as well as vocabulary.

Bajang

The *bajang* is a vampire. According to some traditions, it came from the body of a stillborn child, coaxed out of it by various incantations. It can appear as a stocky human figure with claws and talons or as a wildcat with orange eyes, in this form usually threatening children. The *bajang* can be enslaved and turned into a servant and is often handed down from one generation to the next within a family. Kept in a bamboo vessel, it is fed with milk and eggs. Its master can send the *bajang* out to inflict harm on his enemy, who dies from a mysterious disease.

Baju Melayu

Translated literally as "Malay shirt", this refers to the traditional Malay attire of the males. It consists of a loose long-sleeved shirt (*baju*) with a round collar and a pair of loose pants (*seluar*). On ceremonial or formal occasions, a short *sarung*, reaching down to the knees, known as *kain samping*, is wrapped over the pants. The *samping* can range from a simple wrap-around skirt, (*kain sarung*) to one made of *sungkit* material. *Baju Melayu* is generally made of plain material in a wide range of colours, the fanciest of them being seen during special occasions such as Hari Raya and weddings. The shirt and trousers are complemented with a *songkok*. The *baju Melayu* set seems to have had an interesting genesis, with Indian as well as Chinese influences having gone into it.

Young boy in *baju Melayu*.
(Photo by Fiona Wong)

Balai

A *balai* is the place where community leaders gather for meetings or where rituals are held as in the past from the earliest days of the region's history. In the early days before the establishment of the sultanates, when local dignitaries were in power, their official homes, known as *kedatuan*, had separate adjacent structures known as *balai*. Later, the *balai* became a part of a palace as the *balai rong*. This was the public hall in which dignitaries, officials and the general population would pay homage or respects to the ruler. Official rites and ceremonies take place in the *balai*. In the Minangkabau areas, a *balai* is called *balai adat*. The *balai* has many variations both in style of construction and usage. The *balai panca persada*, for instance was once used for the ceremonial bathing (*bersiram tabal*) of a ruler before his coronation, with all accompanying rites and ceremonies (*adat istiadat*).

In tandem with the development of Malay culture and social life, various types of *balai* have come into use. These include *balai penanggah*, an open shed where food is prepared during a wedding and *balai pengantin*, where a newly married couple sit for their official meal with members of their respective families, close relatives and friends. During the past several decades, large halls, known as *balai* or *dewan* (from Arabic meaning hall) have come into use for public gatherings. These are exemplified by *dewan masyarakat*, or public assembly halls, as well as large halls in hotels, public buildings or university campuses. One of the most familiar current uses of the term *balai* is in *balai polis* or police station.

Balai in a traditional healing performance in Kelantan, Malaysia. (Photo by Ghulam-Sarwar Yousof)

Balik Kampung

Balik kampung literally means to return one's native village (*kampung*) or town. This is a traditional phenomenon when young and old, particularly the young, leave the towns and cities where they live or work and head in droves to their hometowns or where their elders live to celebrate a festival. Although such movements or homeward returns takes place during school holidays, public holidays as well as long weekends, the *balik kampung* phenomenon is particularly connected with *Eid-al-Fitr* or Hari Raya Puasa, the festival that marks the end of the month-long fast of Ramadan. The annual exodus from Kuala Lumpur is particularly marked at this time, comparable to only to that which takes place for Chinese New Year celebrations.

There are similar events in other countries, notable examples being Bangladesh and the Philippines, involving the return home (*balik bayan*) of large numbers of expatriate workers for Christmas or the New Year. However, in some ways, the Malaysian *balik kampung* is a unique phenomenon, even if not comparable in scale to some of the others, due to its multiracial and multicultural character.

Bangsawan

Bangsawan is a form of urban popular theatre which came into being in Penang in the 1880s as a result of the imitation of the Urdu/Hindustani Parsi theatre staged by a visiting company from Bombay, India. Performed by multiracial groups, it spread from Penang to Singapore, parts of Indonesia as well as into Thailand.

Bangsawan has a very large repertoire of stories, Eastern as well as Western, originally taken over from the Parsi theatre. Following independence in 1957, concerted efforts were made to turn *bangsawan* into a "Malay" theatre form with the inclusion of stories with local settings that highlighted Malay values.

A *bangsawan* performance consists of several scenes, each separated by the drop of a curtain. Dances, songs and music from various communities, comedy skits or acrobatics were at one time presented within a performance or between scenes as extra-turns. With the increasing influence of Islam, however, these have become almost non-existent. Today, their place is generally taken by songs or comic skits.

Bangsawan was superseded by modern drama and especially by the Malay cinema which began to develop in the 1930s. It declined after the Second World War, but did not entirely die out. Occasional performances, with some innovations, may still be seen from time to time, particularly in Kuala Lumpur.

Scene from a *bangsawan* performance.
(Photo by Ghulam-Sarwar Yousof)

Batu Surat Terengganu

Batu Surat Terengganu, or The Terengganu Stone, is regarded as the most important evidence so far unearthed for the introduction of Islam into the Malay Peninsula. The *hijri* date on the stone, AH 702, corresponds to 1303 CE. Historically, it is significant for it predates the conversion of the first ruler of Malacca to Islam by at least a century.

The stone measures 84 cm in length with a maximum breadth of 53 cm and an average depth of 24 cm, weighing 214.8 kilograms. It was unearthed from a river bed in 1887 and placed at a prayer house (*surau*) in Kampung Buluh near Kuala Berang, approximately 40 kilometres upstream from Kuala Terengganu. It was moved to the Raffles Museum in Singapore, and then placed in the National Museum in Kuala Lumpur before being finally transferred to the Terengganu State Museum.

The script in which the inscription has been written is Arabic. The style of the script indicates that it may have been copied from that used by Muslims in Champa. However, the Terengganu Stone is the first evidence indicating the use of the Arabic script to write the Malay language in Southeast Asia. Before that, Tamil, Dewanagari and Kawi scripts were used.

Batu Surat Terengganu monument in
Terengganu, Malaysia. (Photo by Fiona Wong)

Berjamu

The *berjamu* is a highly elaborate ceremony or ritual usually held with the purpose of appeasing spirits or other invisible beings, particularly following some general illness or in traditional theatre genres—such as *mak yong, menora* or *wayang kulit* in Kelantan, and *mek mulung* in Kedah—for the initiation of an artist. *Berjamu* may also be held on the occasion of *puja pantai*, or ceremonies to appease the spirits (*hantu* or *jin*) of the sea. The more elaborate *berjamu* involves, apart from the invocations (*mantera*) and standard offerings as in the lesser *semah* rite, the sacrifice or animals such as cows, buffalos and goats, which are offered to invisible entities. In *berjamu* held in conjunction with traditional theatre, both for convenience as well as to avoid controversy, no live animals are used; in their place, images of animals made of flour and so on are used as substitutes. All offerings are placed in a *balai* or "palace" made of bamboo, allowing them to be "consumed" by spirits arriving through the trance of a *bomoh*. Following the several rites and ceremonies, the *balai* and the complete set of offerings are taken to be deposited at places, such as forests and seas, where the spirits are believed to have their homes.

Scene from a *berjamu* ritual performance. (Photo by Ghulam-Sarwar Yousof)

Bersanding

The religious ceremony which marks a Muslim wedding is the *akad nikah*. However, in Malay weddings, the more glamorous event is usually the *bersanding* or *upacara persandingan*, the sitting-in-state ceremony, when the bride and bridegroom sit together on a decorated dais (*pelamin*) to be blessed by elders and guests. The *bersanding* has parallels with a South Indian Hindu rite also held during a marriage. It may take place immediately following the *akad nikah* or at some later more convenient date together with the feast (*kenduri*) or reception. For the *bersanding*, the bridegroom arrives in a procession to the bride's house. The procession could include musicians playing *kompang* frame-drums or singing *hadrah* songs. On arrival, the bridegroom takes his place on the *pelamin* beside the bride. A tiered tray (*astakona*) is placed in front of the pelamin, with each tier containing a mound of cooked yellow rice studded with red-dyed eggs.

The parents of both the bride and groom, senior members of the families and guests "bless" the couple by spraying water laced with incense from a brass censer upon on them or on their open palms, as well as placing a pinch of shredded and scented leaves. They also feed the couple with a tiny amount of sugar or sweets. Due to its pre-Islamic origins and certain animistic elements connected with fertility within it, *bersanding* has in recent decades been discouraged by orthodox Malay Muslims.

Bersemah

Bersemah is a traditional ritual intended to make peace or come to be on terms of amity with invisible beings (*makhluk ghaib*) so that they do not cause any problems to human beings. The *bersemah* is found in many Malay communities with different names in different locations. In Kelantan, this ritual is known as *berjamu*. The ritual is based upon Malay beliefs regarding spirits (*hantu*) and their ability to disrupt the peaceful life of a community. The *bersemah* is conducted by a *bomoh* or *pawang*. The most important elements are invocations (*mantera*) addressed to the invisible entities and the making of food offerings to them. In a minor *bersemah*, these consist of a roasted chicken (*ayam panggang*), yellow glutinous rice (*pulut kuning*), eggs and water.

Bersiram

Bersiram, from the basic word *siram* (to sprinkle) implies the sprinkling of anything with water, such as in watering plants, but also in terms of the cultural practices, the ceremonial sprinkling of anything with holy water. It also means to bathe. *Bersiram*, then, is a cleaning or bathing ceremony. There are many occasions on which such a ceremony takes place. These include weddings, coronations and so on, particularly involving nobility. In traditional theatre, *bersiram* takes place upon the completion of ritual (*berjamu*) performances. Seven pots of water containing croton leaves and other offerings are used either for a full a bath, for the washing of the face and limbs or for drinking. Principally, participants such as a leading *mak yong* actors or a puppeteer (*dalang*) usually take a full bath. It is believed that *bersiram* removes any malicious influence (*badi*) that may subsist as a result of contact with supernatural forces who invariably play a part in spiritual theatre performances.

Bidadari

Bidadari (from Sanskrit *vidhya dharya* 'bearer of knowledge'), is a Malay-Indonesian term that, in keeping with Indian concepts, refers to heavenly maidens living in the celestial palace of the god Indra. In Hindu and Buddhist mythology, *bidadari* are also known as *apsara* or *apsarasa*, female spirits of the clouds and waters. The belief in *bidadari* and certain other classes of mythological beings reached Southeast Asia with Hindu and Buddhist culture in the early centuries CE.

Bidadari figures appear principally in traditional Malay literature, translations of Indian literature or in folklore. Basically, they still keep their Indian names with slight variations or distortions. These include Sekerba, Sargandi or Seri Kandi, Nila Kendi and Nila Utama. They are represented as kindly fairies or as presiding genie at the union of lovers. Another source of the belief lies in popular Islamic romances such as *Indra Sabha*, translated into Malay as *Syair Indera Sabaha*. In these works, the designation changes from *bidadari* to the Persian *peri* or Urdu *pari*. Their names, too, change accordingly.

Following the spread of Islam in Indonesia and Malaysia, *bidadari* came to be identified with heavenly maidens, *houri*, mentioned in the Holy Quran. As a general term, the term *bidadari* is also used to refer to any beautiful woman, usually with the suggestion that she descended from heaven (*kayangan*).

Bidan

Derived from Sanskrit (*widwan*), a *bidan* is a midwife, usually called respectfully as *tok bidan* or *mak bidan*. A midwife is usually engaged in advance with a retaining fee. Further payments consist of fee for services rendered as well as presents and an invitation to a feast on the patient's complete recovery.

In traditional literature and theatre, the *bidan* comes not alone but with six others, comprising the seven midwives (*bidan tujuh*), the number seven being some kind of a magical or mystical number, also seen in seven craftsmen (*tukang tujuh*), seven warriors (*pahlawan tujuh*) and so on. This idea of the youngest (*bongsu*) being the most important, the most beautiful etc., appears in other cultures as well, especially in fairy tales.

Bomoh

The *bomoh*, also known by various other names including *pawang* and *dukun*, is the traditional medicine-man or healer, usually but not necessarily male. For convenience of discussion, it is possible to include the many varieties of *bomoh* into three main categories according to their activities, the first being the external *bomoh* (*bomoh luaran*) who deal with external physical ailments such as broken limbs. To the second category belong *bomoh* with expertise in magic rites connected with matters related to love and hate. Then, there are *bomoh* who can cause good or harm on the request of their clients. Here, too, belong the *bomoh* who indulge in fishing and agriculture magic. Thirdly, there are *bomoh*, *pawang* or *dukun* (*bomoh dalaman*) who deal with emotional, spiritual or psychological illnesses, as well as those resulting from possession by evil spirits. Such a *bomoh* would then be a Malay shaman who is in touch with denizens of the invisible world, able to communicate with them, and to negotiate with them on behalf of his patients, often from a position of superiority due to his knowledge of religion as well as the occult, mastery of spiritual texts as well as the ability to conduct ritual practices often involving trance. Such *bomoh* are usually described according to particular genres or types of healing methods: *bomoh belian*, *bomoh bagih*, *bomoh puteri* and so on.

Despite modernisation and the spread of modern medicine, the *bomoh* or *pawang* is a permanent element in the life of an average Malay from almost any class.

Bomoh at a theatre performance making offerings.
(Photo by Ghulam-Sarwar Yousof)

Borea

Borea or *boria*, is a form of sing-song performance with limited dance usually done by troupes consisting of men or women or by mixed-gender groups. It is believed to have developed from the Iranian passion play (*taziya*) connected with tragic events that befell the family of Prophet Muhammad soon after he passed away in 632 A.D. These have to do with the death of Ali, the prophet's son-in-law and Islam's fourth caliph and as well as those of Ali's sons, Hassan and Hussein. Hussein was killed at Kerbala, close of Kufa, by followers of Yazid, son of Muawiyah on the 10th day of Muharram, the first month of the Muslim calendar in 680 AD. This is most tragic single event staged in *taziya*.

Taziya was introduced into Penang in the late 19th century by north Indian Muslims belonging to the Indian Sepoy regiments. Early performances included parades, with participants wearing sack-cloth garments, strolling minstrels singing tragic songs connected with the martyrdom at Kerbala, and carts with model tombs (*tabut*) drawn along the streets. These culminated in night-time theatre performances, details of which have been lost.

During the first century of its existence, *taziya*, renamed *borea*, shifted away from ritual to entertainment, becoming an altogether new performance genre, with some elementary theatre activity in the form of humorous sketches not in any way connected with Islam.

Modern *borea* contains no ritual element or dramatic content. Typically, it is a choric performance with a composer of the lyrics (*tukang karang*) reciting the more significant poetic passages. Splendidly dressed, he is accompanied by a dozen artists—male, female or mixed—known as sailors, constituting the chorus. The especially composed lyrics are sung to tunes borrowed from Western, Malay and Hindustani popular music while the steps are based upon popular Western dances. Presentations serve the functions of social criticism, providing humour. Extolling dignitaries or praising the government for particular achievements. These days, public performances are rarely seen, while competitions, involving a number of groups, occasionally take place. As a genre, *borea* has not moved outside Penang.

Bota

Bota (from the Sanskrit *bhuta*) is a giant, similar to *raksasa* of Hindu mythology. Such characters, usually physically ugly, often multi-headed and multi-armed, and by nature evil, appear in traditional literature, both folk as well as classical, as well as, through the use of mythological as well as epic materials, in traditional theatre. There is a whole range of such figures, male as well as female, without actual categorization into types or groups. One of the most prominent is the demon king Rawana (Ravana), referred to as a *Bota* King, who is the antagonist of Seri Rama, the noble prince in the *Ramayana*. A particularly interesting female figure is Tuan Puteri Bota, the ogre princess in the *mak yong* story *Raja Tangkai Hati*. These *bota* and *rakshasa*, generally living in the wilds of nature and associated with certain localities, are quite indistinguishable from the *gergasi*, possibly a local term, and the three terms are often quite indistinguishable and used interchangeably. In literature as well as popular usage, these terms are regarded as pre-Islamic, with the Arabic term *jin* taking their place in more recent writings with a somewhat broadened usage.

Bota character from a *mak yong* performance.
(Photo by Ghulam-Sarwar Yousof)

Buka Panggung

Buka panggung is a term that refers to rituals which prepare the traditional theatre buildings or spaces for performances of most genres of traditional theatre. They involve the use of invocations addressed to various categories of spirits as well as the making of offerings to them. The intention is to appease the spirits and to gain their goodwill, so that performances can take place without any problem or disturbance. The *buka panggung* rituals are usually conducted by a qualified bomoh.

Theatre opening ritual in *main puteri* performance.
(Photo by Ghulam-Sarwar Yousof)

Bulan Puasa

Literally meaning the fasting month, this is the popular Malay name for the Muslim month of Ramadan during which Muslims all over the world observe fasting from dawn to evening. Among the Malays, a clear distinction may be in the manner in which Ramadan is marked in the villages as compared to the cities. Among wealthy and middle-class urban Malays, despite the dictate that fasting during Ramadan be taken seriously with a considerable reduction in the consumption of food and other benefits that would stimulate the appetite, the month often turns into a period of luxurious eating with huge menus of delectable foods offered in luxury hotels in the country's major towns and cities for the breaking of the fast (*buka puasa*) time at sunset.

Apart from the connection with food, the second half of Ramadan becomes a period of intense shopping and preparation for the feast of *Eid-ul-Fitr* (Hari Raya Puasa) which takes place on the first of the new month of Shawal, following the sighting of the new moon, to mark the end the month-long fast, marked by the celebration of Hari Raya Puasa or *Eid-dul-Fitr*. Food-stalls, selling traditional and modern cakes, glutinous rice (*pulut*) cooked in bamboo, known as lemang, boiled rice wrapped in leaves (*ketupat*) and dry spicy beef (*rendang*), as well as other items, particularly clothing, mushroom in what have come to be known as Bazaar Ramadan. Similarly, shopping centres stock items of clothing suitable for the occasion. Interestingly, the ardent shoppers include sizeable numbers of non-Muslims, given, in particular, the fact that unusual food items as well as traditional cakes (*kuih*) may be obtained. Special decorations especially created for *Bulan puasa*, include plastic or paper symbols of the moon and star. In mosques throughout the country, congregational prayers (*tarawih*) are held every evening during the month.

Bumiputera

*Bumipute*ra is a compound world made up of two Sanskrit words: *bumi* for earth and *putera* for son or, in courtly language, scion of a royal or princely house. The word in Malaysia is used to refer to sons of the soil, or natives of the country. Strictly speaking, it refers to who are not Malays, since the Malays are placed in a separate category due to their religion, which is Islam. Thus, the *Bumiputera* are the aboriginals (*orang asli*) as well as the various indigenous communities of Sabah and Sarawak. Needless to say, in practical usage in the country, these terms have often cause some confusion, especially when the terms Melayu and *Bumiputera* are used together, or when the term *Bumiputera* (as in the *Bumiputera* policy) seems to apply more to the Malays than even to the natives, such as those from various communities in Sabah and Sarawak.

Bunga Emas

Bunga emas, literally golden flowers, also referred to as *bunga mas bunga perak,* literally golden and silver flowers, was a kind of gift or offering sent by Malay rulers of Kedah, Kelantan, Terengganu and Patani to the king of Thailand as a symbol of his authority over the Malay states. The history of sending *bunga emas* goes back to the 14th century, but became an established practice in the 17th century. According to oral tradition, Kelantan first sent *bunga emas* to Thailand during the reign of Sultan Muhammad II, as a means of expressing gratitude to the Siamese king for recognizing him as the sultan of Kelantan. Terengganu began to send *bunga emas* to Thailand during the reign of Sultan Mansur Syah (1784-1789) in return for assistance received to defeat Ligor. Following the defeat of Patani by the Siamese in 1785, that kingdom too was forced to send *bunga emas* each year to Thailand as a sign of loyalty of its rulers to the Thai king although, in general, *bunga emas* were sent by the Malay rulers once in three years.

Overall, the completed *bunga* mas was created in the form of a flowering tree with branches and twigs at different levels, reaching a height of not less than 1.8 metres. The stem of the tree was made of *cengal* wood wrapped in flattened gold and silver. The vertical stem had four branches to which were attached leaves made of high quality gold and silver, flattened thin like the leaves of the henna plant, and approximately 2.5 cm in length. Each of the branches had three twigs (*ranting*) and each of these had four leaves. To the end of each twig was attached a bunch of four flowers. Usually at the top of the entire tree was placed the symbol of a *burung merbok.* The original value of the golden tree differed from one state to another, depending upon wealth and population size. The *bunga emas* from Kedah was valued at $1500.00 while that from Patani was valued at $1000.00. The *bunga emas* were taken to Bangkok by boat, together with four spears, their upper sections wrapped in gold, a *keris,* and other ceremonial items. In return, the king of Siam gave certain gifts, including rice and salt.

Bunga Rampai

Bunga rampai, literally various mixed flowers, is made up of a combination of various types of beautifully smelling flowers, as well as strips of *daun pandan* and *daun limau perut*, with the addition of rose water, perfumes, sandalwood powder and other items. *Bunga rampai* features as an essential item in several different ceremonies, including *bersanding*, circumcisions, shaving ceremonies for children and maulud gatherings marking the birthday of Prophet Muhammad (*maulud-un-Nabi*). During a *bersanding*, a pinch of such mixed flowers and leaves is placed on the hands of both the bride and the groom by well-wishers. *Bunga rampai*, with a candle, is placed in the bridal chamber following a wedding ceremony to make the room delicately perfumed.

Burung Petalawati

Burung Petalawati is a bird mentioned in old stories as a guardian of the state of Kelantan. It appeared in a *sultan*'s dream. The bird has been described as a mythical creature which served as the vehicle of the god Shiva. It is said that large numbers of such birds, flying in Kelantan skies, saved the state from disaster and also gave the assurance of protection in case of attacks by enemies. Based on the dream, Sultan Mohammed IV ordered that models of the bird be constructed for processions to mark the circumcisions of his sons in 1923 and 1933. Two huge birds were constructed in 1923 and given the names Petala Indera and Candera Wati. The princes who rode on the birds were dressed in silk, wore ceremonial crowns, golden jewellery as well as *Keris*. As a record of these events, the national museum in Malaysia built a smaller-scale model of *Burung Petalawati* for display in its cultural section.

C

Caping

Caping are modesty discs used by children. *Caping* used by young girls have floral designs while those meant for boys have simpler designs, usually cross-like. *Caping* were used by Indians as well as Malays on the east coast of the Malay Peninsula, as well as in Sri Lanka, Vietnam, Cambodia, Thailand and the Philippines. In Malaysia, the use of *caping* became a customary practice, at times involving a ceremony done by a bomoh. *Caping* went out of use from around the 1920s and may, these days, be seen only in private collections or in museums.

A *caping.* (Sketch by Fiona Wong)

Cerita Penglipur Lara

Literally stories told to please the unhappy, *cerita panglipur lara* were traditional tales usually handed down in an oral tradition through itinerant story-tellers (*tukang cerita*). Usually presented in the evenings in rural communities when villagers had time to rest from their labours and go on late into the nights, with the longer stories taking several nights to be completed.

A *penglipura lara* story, usually combining tragic and comic elements with fantasy, would generally be set in well-known kingdom. The stories were presented in rhythmic prose or verse, including *pantun*, at times to the accompaniment of musical instruments. The best known style of storytelling in this manner is *awang batil*, which is still active. Two others, *selampit* and *tarik selampit*, are rarely seen.

Cerita Panji

The medieval Javanese Panji cycle of romances is based upon the wanderings, adventures and romance of Raden Inu Kertapati, more popularly known as Sri Panji or Inu/Inao, and his fiancée, Raden Galuh Cendera Kirana, a princess of Daha. Originating in Central Java, the stories spread to other parts of Southeast Asia from the Majapahit period during the political and cultural expansion of Java, gaining popularity both as literary texts as well as serving to provide some of the material for the visual as well as performing arts. In the Indonesian islands, literary versions of Panji stories spread in Javanese, as well as in the languages of Sumatra, Sulawesi and Lombok. In similar fashion, the tales spread to the Malay Peninsula as well as to the countries in northern Southeast Asia, including Thailand, Cambodia and Myanmar, finding a significant place both as literature and as sources for the performing arts following various degrees of localization.

In the Malay language, Panji stories have been written in the form of prose as *hikayat,* as well as verse (*syair*). The major *hikayat* include *Hikayat Cekel Waneng Pati, Hikayat Panji Kuda Semirang* and *Hikayat Panji Semirang.* Connections between these and Indonesian versions have been traced by scholars. In the syair form, well-known Panji stories include *Syair Ken Tambuhan, Syair Lelakon Mesa Kumitar* and *Syair Panji Semirang.* Apart from the literary versions, selected Panji stories were at one time featured in the Malay *wayang kulit* Melayu, a form of shadow play active in Kelantan, which has become extinct. They continue to be used in various dance creations.

D

Dabus

Dabus is a form of ritual dance active in various parts of Sumatra in Indonesia as well as in Selangor and southern Perak in Malaysia. It is believed that it originated in the Middle East or in Persia. In the Arabic language, the word *dabus* refers to a stick or sharp pin or dagger-like instrument, *anak dabus*, used by the dancers. *Dabus* is said to have been used by early Muslims during battles against non-Muslims. The sword-fighting skills, the ability to withstand the pain of being pelted with stones, burnt with fire, or pierced with sharp metal skewers are believed to have come from a combination of supernatural power and the special ability to develop physical resistance.

It is believed that *dabus* was introduced into the Malay world by one Syed Ahmad bin Ali Hassan al-Rifal from Baghdad. Three varieties are known: *dabus kebal*, *dabus berdarah* and *dabus gubahan*. The first and second, like the original *dabus*, are serious in nature while the third, emphasizing dance elements, has been developed as an art form for presentation at public gatherings such as weddings and welcoming ceremonies.

The principal instrument is the *anak dabus* or *damak*. This is a short, spear-shaped weapon made of metal or cane, about 25 to 35 centimeters long and with a handle. Metal rings attached to the handle provide a rhythm when the dancers move in specific steps in harmony with the *rebana*. The *anak dabus* is used by the dancers to pierce their own arms at certain stages during a performance, particularly when they are in a state of trance.

The principal musical instruments are frame-drums (*rebana*), barrel-drums (*gendang*) and a pair of hanging gongs. The number of *rebana* and *gendang* is variable. The *dabus* musical repertoire consists of about a dozen pieces, including several named after members of the family of the Ali, Islam's fourth Caliph.

Performances, lasting from several minutes to a couple of hours, commence with theatre consecration rituals and the singing of religious songs (*nasyid*) to musical accompaniment. Dancers then enter with their *anak dabus*, shaking them to create a rhythmic sound. Standard dance steps take them back and forth as well as in tiny circles. After some time, trance takes place and, using the *anak dabus*, the dancers pierce themselves in the arms until blood begins to flow.

A young *dabus* performer from Teluk Intan, Perak, Malaysia. (Photo by Ghulam-Sarwar Yousof)

Dalang

Originally a Javanese word meaning story-teller as in the genres *dalang jemplung, dalang kentrung* and so on, it is best known as referring to the puppeteer of the shadow play, *wayang kulit*, and the theatre style using doll-like puppets, *wayang golek*. In Java, there are several categories of puppeteers, depending upon expertise and experience. This is not the case in Malaysia. The *dalang*, in Kedah and Kelantan where *wayang kulit* is performed, act as story-tellers, who, while developing the narrative of the story, also provide voices for all characters represented by the puppets. In addition, they conduct the necessary rituals for performances of the *wayang* as well as guide musicians.

Puppeteer (*dalang*) performing the shadow play in
Kelantan, Malaysia. View inside the theatre.
(Photo by Ghulam-Sarwar Yousof)

Daulat

When it comes to the origin and consolidation of Malay royalty, two key ideas seem to have come coalesced: the Hindu-Buddhist concept cult of the god-king (*devaraja*) and that of kingship from Persia.

The *devaraja* cult was highly influential in Southeast Asian countries during the period of Hinduism, with its fullest expression seen in Angkor and other early Cambodian cities. Essentially, this gave the local kings the status of gods. There is no clear indication that the *devaraja* cult was as powerful in the early Malay sultanates as it was in Indonesia and Cambodia. Such a concept appears to have been absent from the Middle East and it certainly does not find a place in Islamic thinking. The closest that one comes to such a concept is that of the special power or energy (*barakah*) of prophets (*nabi, rasul*) and saints (*wali*). This is usually translated as charisma (*keramat*) or blessing rather than suggesting anything supernatural, and is in fact closer to the concept of *daulat* with its implication that to royalty belongs some sort of superior status, without the status of caste, such as Kshatriya in India, a class to which Hindu kings belonged.

The possession of *daulat*, nevertheless, suggests the presence of a certain special power or energy (*sakti*) which, in the case of Malay rulers, assumes a shade or quality different from Brahmins as well as with those in possession of magical powers, such healers or shamans (*bomoh*). The origin of the term "*sultan*" as well as the concept of *daulat* came from Persia, possibly with the South Asian sub-continent serving as an intermediary. The name Shah, commonly adopted by Malay rulers, also has its origins in Persia.

Derhaka

From Sanskrit (*droha* or *droha-ka*) also Old Javanese Kawi (*drohaka*), this word firstly means disobedience, disloyalty or treason to a ruler or to the State itself. The second meaning of the word includes disobedience to the lawful authority of an official superior, or parents as well as of going against customary conduct. In the case of a woman, *derhaka* also includes infidelity or disobedience to her husband. In the case of *derhaka* against the ruler or the State, the punishment was the same as indicated in the entry *murka*. The full implications of the word *derhaka* may still be seen in Malay communities, even though the ultimate punishment is rarely meted out. There have, for instance, been cases where official titles (*anugerah*) have been withdrawn from persons believed to have committed *derhaka*.

Dewa

The word *dewa* (Sanskrit *deva*), the concepts behind it as well as mythology associated with it entered Malay culture with Hinduism from India, possibly through Java. It appears that before the use of this word, *dewa* or *dewata* for gods, there was none to describe higher deities. This raises interesting questions regarding the beliefs of the Malays at that point in time. In the end, there came about a belief in a fairly large number of gods (*dewa*) and goddesses (*dewi*), including Dewa Bisnu (Vishnu) and Dewa Betara Guru (Shiva). When it comes to particular usage, the word *dewata* occurs, in its most elevated sense, in the name Dewata Mula Raya, meaning the first and original God.

Apart from important roles in mythology, *dewa* figures have also found important places in the epics, particularly the *Ramayana*, an important source of dramatic repertoire in the shadow play (*wayang kulit*). It is also notable that apart from the development of the *dewa*-concept indicated above, there exists another set of *dewa*, as yet unidentified, occurring in traditional literature, theatre and in healing rituals, particularly in Kelantan and Patani. Most prominent in this respect are the twelve *dewa* characters in the *mak yong* dance theatre and in the *main puteri* shaman dance.

Dewi

Dewi, from the Sanskrit *devi*, is the female counterpart of *dewa* (god), meaning goddess. Its usage entered Malay culture through Indonesia, where the terms may have come into use as early as the 2nd century AD, with the arrival of Hinduism and Indian culture. Following the spread of Hinduism, several goddesses seem to have gained prominence among the Malays, with *Dewi* as a name referring to the consort of Shiva. The name Mahadewi (the great goddess), also apparently referring to the same figure is also known, while Shakti appears to have been used as a proper name, as well as a general symbol for divine female power, possibly from the idea of Shakti as the female energy of Shiva.

In the *Ramayana* translated into Malay when used in such contexts as the traditional theatre, the designation *Dewi* remains even if the first part of the female name gets changed or localized, as in Siti Dewi. On the human level, *Dewi*, as in the case of Indian Hindus, also commonly occurs as part of a name in Indonesia, but not among the Malays.

Dikir Barat

Dikir barat is a form of lyrical verse debate involving group singing active principally in Kelantan and in southern Thailand. It may be performed without music or with percussion instruments. *Dikir barat* is believed to have developed in southern Thailand from *zikir* or Islamic songs. It is performed by groups of between 10 and 15 members with a leader named *juara* or *tok juara*. The other members of a troupe serve as a chorus (*awok-awok*). Performers usually sit cross-legged on a platform or stage. Traditionally done in rural or semi-rural communities of Kelantan, this genre has spread widely throughout west Malaysia with government support as well as in Singapore. Performances take place for entertainment or in situations involving competitions. National competitions have been broadcast on radio and television since 1993 and there has been some encouragement to present performances with lyrics in the English language.

The creative leader of a *dikir barat* group is the tukang karut. Leading the chorus members, his recital includes quatrains known as *pantun*, many of which are improvised. These may touch upon everyday life but the *tukang karut* may also address social issues, politics, government policies as well as touch upon human foibles in his lyrics, often with the addition of clapping, side-to-side swaying and other rhythmic body movements by chorus members, building up to crescendo. *Dikir barat* has traditionally been a male preserve but in recent years, especially in urban areas, female *dikir barat* groups have emerged. In competition, the *tukang karut* of one group will open a topic with a question, the *awok-awok* will respond to him and the *tukang karut* of the opposing group will respond, in what then develops into a battle of wits.

Dunia Melayu

In a cultural or symbolic sense, the phrase *dunia Melayu* refers to the "Malay world". This is a term without any validity in a geographical sense. However, for the Malays it seems to represent some vague and undefined notion of land(s) in which the Malay language and, to some extent, "Malay" culture appear to be significant, colouring the lives of the people. Malay writers would like to believe that *alam Melayu*, a variant expression to *dunia Melayu*, includes vast lands stretching beyond territories actually inhabited by Malays. It may be more appropriate to think of this in terms of a diaspora, once again from the perspective of the Malaysian Malay rather than from the vastly different Indonesian perspective for, in actuality, the term Indonesian diaspora is far more appropriate, considering the possible origins of the Malays themselves as a small community in Sumatra.

G

Gamelan Melayu

Gamelan is the name of an orchestra which, in most instances and in various sizes, accompanies the performances of most classical and folk theatre genres in Indonesia. A complete *gamelan* orchestra may have in it up to about 20 different types of instruments, the instruments themselves numbering more than 70. They include metallophones, drums and a *rebab*. These are divided into two different scales (*pelog* and *slendro*). Usually, however, only one of these scales in used so that, apart from its use in the highly elaborate court traditions of dance, the complete *gamelan* set is seldom used. The *gamelan* was brought into Pahang through a royal marriage between the court of Riau-Lingga in Indonesia and Pahang and another in the 20th century between the courts of Pahang and Terengganu, together with its specific musical repertoire and dances. This unique style of *gamelan* came to be known as *gamelan Melayu* and the dance known as *joget gamelan* developed as forms distinct from those in Indonesia.

Gergasi

The *gergasi*, a tusked cannibal, is a gigantic figure living in forests. He plays a considerable part in Malay folktales. According to local tradition, as preserved in *Hikayat Merong Mahawangsa* (or *The Kedah Annals*), the original inhabitants of Kedah were *gergasi*. They intermarried with the first human settlers and, owing to this intermarriage, a later Kedah Sultan grew tusks and developed a taste for human blood.

Two other types of such figures are *bota* (from Sanskrit *bhuta*) and *raksasa* (from Sanskrit *rakshasa*). The differences between them are not very clear. Generally, they are seen as not evil. Raksasa are known in Hindu mythology as well as epic literature; it is through these sources that they entered Malay mythology and literature.

Ghazal

Ghazal is a form of vocal and instrumental music performed principally in the state of Johor. The term *ghazal* itself comes from an Arabic form of poetry which, originating in the 8th century, expanded considerably in Persia as well as northern India in the Persian and Urdu languages, both at the popular level as well as under royal patronage in the Muslim courts. In India and Pakistan, the *ghazal* in Urdu continues as the most popular form of lyrical poetry to this day, manifested in poetry gatherings (*mushairah*) as well as in films with the involvement of established poets.

Among the Malays the term *ghazal* refers to a form of musical rather than literary expression. There are two styles of *ghazal* today: *ghazal party* (where party means group) which is active in the northern part of the country and *ghazal Melayu* found in Johor. The former uses Arab or Middle Eastern style of music. *Ghazal Melayu*, on the other hand, is based upon Persian and North Indian (Hindustani) music. This form is believed to have developed in Riau-Lingga in the early 19th century and introduced into Johor from that part of Indonesia.

Ghazal Melayu makes use of the following Middle Eastern, Indian and western instruments: harmonium, tabla, viola, gambus, guitar, tambourine and maracas. Malay *pantun* serve as the lyrics while the subject-matter of the *ghazal* includes beauty of natural phenomena; particular locations within the country such as Mersing or Tanjung Puteri; and melancholy or touching tales as well as romance. The lyrics may contain messages intended to inculcate good conduct (*budi*) or serving as a means of advice (*nasihat*). In general, the tone of *ghazal Melayu* tends to be romantic and melancholy.

Gurindam

Gurindam is a type of irregular verse form in traditional Malay poetry. It is made up of a combination of two clauses where the first forms a line and is linked to the second line, regarded as the main clause. A stanza thus consists of two lines which provide together provide a complete idea. They have the same end-rhyme. There is no limit on the number words per line. Neither the rhythm per line is fixed. The first line of a *gurindam* is known as syarat and the second line is jawab. In other words, the first line states a condition while the second provides the answer. One of the best-known works in the *gurindam* style is Gurindam Dua Belas (Twelve Gurindam) of Raja Ali Hajiwritten in 1847.

Guru

From Sanskrit meaning teacher, this word means exactly what is does in the original language. There are, of course, local variations, especially when it comes to be applied in specific contexts. Thus, firstly there is the original meaning implying some kind of relationship between a teacher and a pupil or disciple in a religious sense. In Malay usage, this may be seen to persist when one speaks of a teacher giving religious instruction (*guru ugama*), a teacher of the martial arts called silat (*guru silat*) and so in a wide range of other such applications, often with the appellation or honorific Tok, when a particular name is stated (e.g. Tok Guru Nik Aziz). Alternatively, in such instances, another word, *ustaz* or *ustad*, also known among Muslims of South Asia, comes into use. In its second, broader usage, the word *guru* refers to any teacher, for instance, a schoolmaster; in such cases, again with an appellation Cik, the word changes into Cikgu in common usage.

H

Hadrah

Hadrah refers to two types of performances, the first consisting of laudatory songs and the second a form of theatre in the manner of *bangsawan*, at times named *bangsawan hadrah*. Various opinions suggest its origins of these genes from Hadramaut in the Arabian Peninsula, from India or from Java.

The laudatory variety of *hadrah*, believed to have been derived from the song sung to welcome the Prophet Muhammad and his small entourage into Medina following his migration (*hijrah*) from Mecca, or conversely, to welcome him back into Mecca at his triumphant reentry into that city following his exile. This involves singing to the accompaniment of drumming. The original lyrics consisted of words in praise of God (*Allah*) and the Prophet. While these continue to be used, the lyrics of *hadrah* in Malaysia contain elements derived from both Arab and Indian-Muslim cultures.

Hadrah musical instruments consist only of single-faced drums, *gendang* or *rebana*, in three different sizes. In recent years, a violin is at times included. *Hadrah* recitals take place at weddings in honour of newly-married couples or other special occasions such as welcoming dignitaries or public holidays.

The second variety, known as *bangsawan hadrah*, was once active in the northern and western states of Kedah, Perlis and Perak but is rarely seen these days. A troupe traditionally consisted of 12 men. Contemporary groups, however, have 20 or

Scene from a *hadrah* performance
in Kedah, Malaysia.
(Photo by Ghulam-Sarwar Yousof)

more members including eight dancers, often transvestites. In Kedah and Perlis, the standard *hadrah* musical repertoire consists of 12 musical pieces, sung in an indistinct Arabic-sounding language claimed by performers to be Bengali which in Malaysia normally means Urdu or Hindustani. One of the principal sources of Arabic language lyrics is *Kitab Majmu'at Sharif al-Anam*, better known as *Kitab Berzanji*. In addition, there is a fairly large repertoire of local creations in the Malay language.

Halus and Kasar

In their broader application, these terms—*halus* meaning refined and *kasar* meaning coarse—are usually taken as a pair of contraries. They may apply to material objects, to abstract or intangible entities such as language, to the arts as well as to human character and behaviour. The concept seems to have originated among the Javanese (*alus-kasar*) where it appears in its most sophisticated form and to have spread from Java to neighbouring regions.

Firstly, and most obviously, the terms *halus* and *kasar* describe a wide range of material objects such as textiles, more particularly batik materials. In batik, there is a clear gradation of quality based not just on the type of material used for the production of batik but also the type of workmanship and designs. Batik and silk, while seen in terms of textiles, may also be regarded as art objects, especially when painting or embroidery are featured on them. Shadow play (*wayang kulit*) puppets are similarly classified based upon the characters depicted and the manner in which the puppets are carved and painted, for essentially the figures represent the personalities of the characters. Thus, Seri Rama is the most refined of all characters and Rawana the coarsest.

When it comes to performances, the notion of *halus-kasar* is applicable to dance, music or theatre. Movements of dancers, as well as puppets in *wayang kulit* may be seen as coarse or refined, depending upon how a character moves and speaks. Overall, there is gradation between extreme refinements to extreme coarseness.

Thirdly, when applied to the human species, the term *halus* suggests overall refinement of personality, as well as behaviour, while *kasar* suggests its contrary. To the Malay, refinement is indicated by elegant words, such as those used by members of royalty in official capacities. Both code of conduct and language suggest adherence to etiquette (*adat*), customs and traditions, which derive from indigenous notions of social stratification.

Hang Tuah

Hang Tuah is a legendary Malay warrior who, having come to Melaka from Bentan in Indonesia, is said to have lived during the reign of Sultan Mansur Shah of the Malacca Sultanate in the 15th century. Seen as a great admiral and outstanding warrior, his life and adventures have been recorded in the two greatest Malay literary works, *Sejarah Melayu* and *Hikayat Hang Tuah*. Despite the passage of centuries, Hang Tuah is strongly connected with four companions: Hang Kasturi, Hang Jebat, Hang Lekir and Hang Lekiu. As a symbol of absolute loyalty—one may even say blind loyalty to his ruler—he is, in some ways, the single iconic figure in Malay feudalism.

Hang Tuah continues to be highly popular as an ideal hero, holding an important place in Malay minds even to this day although historians seriously doubt his very existence. His adventures have served as the basis for several plays in both Malay language and English, as well as other media of artistic and literary expression, including film.

Artist impression of *Hang Tuah*.
(Sketch by Fiona Wong)

Hantu

The Malay-Indonesian word *hantu* is an inclusive one which can be translated as spirit. Originating in animism, it is an inclusive term, referring in essence to good or bad spirits in general. Despite this situation, however, in the popular imagination the term seems to refer to negative forces, particularly to various categories of harmful spirits such of those said to bring about disease. It must be established, however, that neutral or harmless spirits constitute an important section of Malay mythology. Due to the fact that literally thousands of spirits (*hantu*) are known and are of invoked by traditional medicine men or shamans (*bomoh*), it may be best to see them in terms of groups in keeping with their functions. Thus, there are the following (a) nature or environmental spirits; (b) guardian spirits of various types; (c) spirits responsible for illnesses; (d) and so on. Following the arrival of Islam into the region, however, the Arabic term *jin* came to denote good spirits while evil spirits were generally referred to as *hantu.* This is still the case to this day.

Hantu Keramat

Hantu Keramat refers to a spirit which lives in a particular locality but is not a threat or nuisance to human beings. On the contrary, it is believed to assist those who come to its place seeking favours. The places with which this spirit is associated include huge boulders, large trees and certain other areas such as road junctions. *Keramat* help people after receiving some offerings such as an egg. Those who receive the favours of *keramat* are said to be able to win lottery prizes or even get great deal of wealth. Generally, it is believed amongst Muslims that approaching *keramat* in this manner is contrary to Islamic teaching.

Harimau Jadian

Harimau jadian is the Malay name for were tiger. The most common superstition concerns the ability of certain human beings to turn themselves into tigers. This belief is based on the assumption that men or women may have supernatural powers enabling them to turn into tigers in which form they prey upon animals and upon fellow human beings. There are many Malay tales about were tigers, some of them featuring the Sakai, others concerning the men from Korinchi, a small state in Indonesia. Some parallels to Chinese stories. In Malaysia, such tales are known in Kelantan, Terengganu and Negeri Sembilan as well as Johor.

The Malays avoid uttering the word *harimau*, or more commonly *rimau*. They believe that if the word is used during the daytime, it will be impressed on the subconscious mind of the tiger, then dreaming in the jungle. Thereafter, they will be in great danger from the animal which will seek them out. Instead of mentioning the word tiger, fancy names like Tok Belang (the striped one) or Si-Pudong (old hairy face) are used for the animal. There is also the belief that a tiger attacks a person from the back rather than from the front because there is on every person's forehead an inscription from the Holy Quran proclaiming the superiority of men over other creatures. Certain passages from the Quran are recited when entering a forest in the belief that this practice will prevent a tiger from attacking them. There are also charms in the Malay language for protection from attacks by tigers.

Hari Raya Haji

Hari Raya Haji is the Malaysian name for the *Eid-ul-Adha* festival marking the completion in Mecca and its vicinities of the essential rituals connected with the pilgrimage of Hajj, one of Islam's main pillars fulfilled each year by several million people from all over the Muslim world. The actual origins and some of the rituals surrounding the Hajj lie in pre-Islamic times, with the practices being traced back to the Prophet Abraham (Nabi Ibrahim). Celebration of the *Eid-ul-Adha* takes place the world over with congregational prayers in mosques in the morning. As in *Eid-ul-Adha*, graves may be visited but the other activities connected with *Hari Raya Haji* are not observed. The principal act after the prayers is the offering of sacrificial animals, in commemoration of the near-sacrifice by Nabi Ibrahim of his elder son Ismail. Muslims sacrifice a suitable animal and distribute the meat as well as cook a portion of it for their own consumption. In Malaysia, there are no celebrations as such for *Hari Raya Haji*, which is thus a much quieter festival than *Hari Raya Puasa* even though, in religious or spiritual terms, *Hari Raya Haji* is a far greater festival.

Hari Raya Puasa

Hari Raya Puasa is celebrated in a lively manner. Preparations begin even before the commencement of annual fasting in the month of Ramadan, with the ordering of clothes and the making of cakes and biscuits; these activities come to a peak during the first week or so of the fasting period, with food and clothing stalls set up in major town and cities in what has come to be known locally as Bazaar Ramadan, ostensibly to sell food for the breaking of the fast. This in fact has become a major activity, drawing large crowds to specially selected locations along the streets and open spaces, as well as a major industry. Shopping centres also pick up the spirit and mood of the festival.

Over radio and television, special programmes are featured and the singing of songs connected with Hari Raya Puasa may be heard. The lyrics emphasize the special nature of Ramadan and the festival itself: the key message is that of repentance and forgiveness. Muslims are exhorted to repent their sins, seek forgiveness from Allah as well as from everyone else during the days of Hari Raya. This implies that one starts the days immediately following Hari Raya on a clean slate. This is something great in principle but which, in practice, rarely takes place. It even sounds hypocritical, particularly if old enmities are kept simmering during Ramadan and promptly renewed after Hari Raya.

On the actual Hari Raya day, confirmed with the announcement of the sitting of the new moon of Shawal by the religious authorities in the country, congregational prayers are held in all major mosques. Following this, *Hari Raya Puasa* becomes essentially a family-based festival. Younger family members pay respects to elders and the important element, as far as children are concerned, is the receiving of monetary gifts (*duit Raya*) from the elders when wishing a good Hari Raya (Selamat Hari Raya). Certain families visit graves of departed relatives, to clean the graves and say prayers for the deceased. The rest of the celebration consists of visits to friends and family members and the principal activity is the consumption of food, consisting of special dishes including *ketupat*, *pulut* and *rendang* meat. A tradition of having "open houses" has been in existence for several decades now, with important personalities from the Governors of the states which have governors, ministers and other senior government officials also organizing open houses during the whole month of Shawal. Thus, technically, *Hari Raya Puasa* is a month-long festival in Malaysia.

Food preparation for Hari Raya Puasa. A scene from Penang, Malaysia.
(Photo by Ghulam-Sarwar Yousof)

Hati

While the word *jantung* refers to the physical heart, *hati* is seen as the seat of feelings or emotions, as well as the place where one's secret thoughts are held: this is the liver rather than the heart. There are many usages for the word *hati*, usually with an additional word before it or following it, to suggest a state of being or emotional state. Examples include: *buah hati* (beloved), *hati sanubari* (the average human heart), *hati sedu* (the troubled or sad heart), *hati sejuk* (the passive one) and *senang hati* (to be pleased).

In a broader sense, *hati* is seen as representative of human nature or character, a person's natural disposition, as in *baik hati*, good-hearted or *murah hati*, generous. In a religious or mystical sense, with another word following *hati*, it acquires other meanings. Thus, *hati salim* is the disposition of a man who leads an honest life; *hati tawajuh* is the person who devotes himself to God or concentrates his thoughts on God; *hati rabbani* is the heart of someone inclined towards mysticism; and *hati nurani* is the heart of someone who has seen the divine light (*nur*). Needless to say, these additional words in these final examples all come from the Arabic.

Hikayat

The term *hikayat*, literally story or narrative, comes from Arabic and in general is used in almost all Muslim countries for an important genre of literature. *Hikayat* are generally written in prose rather than in verse, but verse *hikayat* do exist. The contents of a *hikayat* may be legendary or based upon history. While dozens of *hikayat* are today regarded as part of Malay literature, many of them in fact came through translation or adaptation of Indian, Persia or Middle Eastern originals, Islamic as well as non-Islamic, including *Hikayat Amir Hamzah*, as well as from within Nusantara. Of those from Indonesia, several Panji stories, such as *Hikayat Panji Semirang*, are the most significant, but there are others such as *Hikayat Raja-Raja Pasai*. The most important local *hikayat* are *Hikayat Merong Mahawangsa* and *Hikayat Hang Tuah*. These are in fact the only two *hikayat* that seem to be having local settings and characters. The best known of Indian-derived *hikayat* is *Hikayat Seri Rama*, based on the epic *Ramayana*.

Hikayat Maharaja Wana

The Hindu epic, *Ramayana*, serves as the principal source of dramatic material for much of the traditional theatre of Southeast Asia, where there are several variant versions differing from the best-known version by Valmiki. In Malaysia, there exist two versions. *Hikayat Seri Rama* follows the well-known Valmiki version in Sanskrit, with some variations and attempts at localisation, and the shorter oral version, *Hikayat Maharaja Wana*, in which significant changes have been made to the events and additional characters have been introduced. This version serves as the source for the principal story (*cerita pokok*) of the plot as performed in the Kelantan shadow play (*wayang kulit*). In addition, many secondary or branch stories (*cerita ranting*) have been invented over the years by Kelantanese puppeteers (*dalang*), in some ways continuing the main story but not related to the *Ramayana*. The incidents used are often the result of borrowing of plots, themes and characterization from other sources, including the mediaeval Javanese Panji cycle of stories. Despite the importance of *Hikayat Maharaja Wana*, most puppeteers today merely pick the more exciting episodes dealing, for instance, with the marriage of Seri Rama and Sita Dewi, the abduction of Sita Dewi and her final recovery from Langkapuri by Seri Rama. The branch stories, however, are much more popular.

Hikayat Merong Mahawangsa

Hikayat Merong Mahawangsa, whose author remains unknown, is work based historical events and exists in several versions. Various myths, legends as well as historical events are incorporated into the story.

The purpose of the story appears to be to relate the history of the Kedah royal family. This *hikayat* indicates that the ancestor of the Kedah sultans was Raja Merong Mahawangsa who descended from the king of Rome. It is evident that this is the story of Raja Phra Ong Mahapudisat, the sixth descendant of Raja Merong Mahawangsa. Phra Ong Mahapudisat accepted Islam and changed his name to Sultan Muzafal Shah.

The *hikayat* provides some details regarding the arrival of Islam, the relations between Kedah and Siam as well as the manner in which the *bunga emas* and *bunga perak* was sent to Siam. The last part contains the names of the rulers of Kedah. This is believed to have been added by a copyist on the orders to Sultan Tajuddin Halim Syah in the 1820s. The *hikayat* uses much symbolism as well as satire, for instance, in the famous episode about Raja Bersiung, the descriptive name of a Kedah raja who, having ogre (*gergasi*) blood, developed tusks and cannibal traits.

Hyang

In several Indonesian languages, including Kawi, Javanese, Sundanese and Balinese, *hyang* is an unseen spiritual entity that has supernatural power. The word may thus be translated as unseen or invisible. Widely associated with Balinese Hinduism, it is also been in use elsewhere in Indonesia for more than a millennium. However, this term actually has an older origin: it has its root in indigenous animism and ancestor worship. It is seen as an ancestral spirit or as a divinity. It serves as an honorific along with another word, *Widhi*, so that it becomes *Hyang Widhi* to refer to the concept of God in Balinese native religion, as above and beyond local deities or Hindu gods. It is clear that the Malays adopted the term *hyang* from native cultures of Indonesia, and in turn transformed it into *yang* as in *Sang Yang Tunggal* (the One and Only), with reference to God. Even though the name *hyang* has long been out of use, it is noteworthy that it remains in modern Bahasa Melayu as part of the word *sembahyang* (*sembah+hyang*) meaning worship of *Hyang*. Thus the name *Hyang* implies Allah. With the greater awareness of Islam and Middle Eastern culture among the Malays, the tendency has come in to use *salah,* the Arabic word for prayer instead of *sembahyang*.

I

Istana

The term *istana*, from Sanskrit *astana*, refers to the residence of a Malay ruler. It serves as a symbol of the dignity and power of the sultan or ruler of the State as well as his status. The term *istana* thus indicates the clear difference between the residence of a ruler and his people (*rakyat*). The *istana* serves as the symbolic centre of power as well as the place where ceremonial activities take place. Apart from housing the various sections necessary for a residence, the *istana* also has special areas such as the hall in which ceremonies take place. This is known as the *balairong*. Around a palace are placed various instruments such as canons for the protection of the *istana* complex as well as the royal family. Malay legendary histories, such as *Hikayat Merong Maha Wangsa* and *Sejarah Melayu*, contain detailed descriptions of various palaces from the past, indicating their architectural features, grandeur as well as the nature of the activities that took place in them. Certain old *istana* in Malaysia have been turned into museums.

An old palace named Istana Kenangan in Kuala Kangsar, Perak, Malaysia. Now a royal museum. (Photo by Ghulam-Sarwar Yousof)

J

Jawi

The word *Jawi* is probably of Arab origin (adjective of *Java* or *Jawa*), pertaining to Sumatra and Jawa. It referred to Java in particular and, by implication, to the broader territories of Nusantara. More importantly, *Jawi* is the Malay language written with the use of Arabic alphabet or script. It came into use as a successor to Sanskrit and Pali. The first evidence for the use of the *Jawi* script in the Malay Peninsula is sometimes traced to the Terengganu Stone (*Batu Surat Terengganu*). Without other corroborative contemporary evidence, it is impossible to assess to what extent *Jawi* was used in the peninsula and in Southeast Asia. In addition to its official use in the royal courts, *Jawi* featured prominently in religious as well as literary texts. With the arrival of Western influence through colonization and education, *Jawi* was relegated to village schools (sekolah pondok), with the Malay language eventually adopting the Romanised script in general usage. Technically, the official language, Bahasa Melayu/Malaysia as well as its variant forms of the language in Singapore, Brunei and Indonesia, also make use of the Romanised script, with a common spelling system adopted over the decades since these countries gained independence. Nevertheless, in some of the Malay states, *Jawi* is still in use in public spaces.

Used in combination with other words, the word *Jawi* gains other meanings. For instance, *jawikan* means to translate into Malay; *huruf jawi* is the *Jawi* script; *masuk jawi*, means to be circumcised.

Jawi and *Rumi* signboard of a mosque in Taiping, Perak, Malaysia. (Photo by Ghulam-Sarwar Yousof)

Jawi Peranakan

The *Jawi Peranakan* are, by definition, Malays of Indian Muslim descent, who have become assimilated into Malay society and identify themselves completely with Malay interests, or a sub-group of Malays within the greater Malay society alongside other sub-groups such as the Malays of Arab, Minangkabau, Javanese, Bugis, Acehnese or Thai descent. Another term used for them is *Jawi Pekan* or *Jawi Pakan*. Like the Malays of other ancestries that have long assimilated into the greater Malay community, the *Jawi Peranakan* exhibit a universal Malay culture, yet display traits peculiar to their own particular sub-culture. Today's *Jawi Peranakan* belong to the third to fifth generation descendants of Indian Muslims who settled in Penang from the end of the 18th century. Penang was their original settlement and they are to be found there, as well as in Kedah, Perlis and Kala Lumpur, with many families having moved to that city in recent decades.

Jembalang

Jembalang is the earth spirit. Malays believe that *jembalang* can cause harm to those who disturb them. For this reason, ceremonies are held to invite or call *jembalang* and to provide them with food offerings when work is about to begin for planting of paddy, opening up land for mining or agriculture or laying the foundations of a house. *Jembalang* are believed to cause wounds when the places they stay in are disturbed, or polluted with rubbish. It is believed that *jembalang* are able to manifest themselves in various forms such a cows or buffaloes, with the aim of showing themselves to people and as a reminder when it is time for a ritual to feed them.

Jikey

Jikey is a form of operatic theatre performed by Malay and Thai communities living along the Malaysian-Thai border in the states of Kedah and Perlis. It resembles *bangsawan*. Oral tradition maintains that it was introduced by Indian-Muslim ("Keling" or Bengali) traders. This genre possesses a fairly extensive repertoire of stories consisting of local legends and fairy tales, Thai folk stories and Middle-Eastern tales. Performances, involving 12 to 16 persons in a troupe, including musicians, take place on a simple stage constructed of *attap* and bamboo. The *jikey* orchestra consists of several instruments commonly seen in other Malay and Thai traditional theatre genres. Following theatre opening rituals, a selected number of introductory musical pieces as well as invocationary songs are presented. In these, respects are paid to spirits (*hantu*) of the localities and their permission sought for the performance. A lively signal piece ushers in a Bengali character who dances and sings with the chorus. He provides the audience with details of the upcoming story. The tales of *jikey*, episodic in character, contain many scenes, taking several hours to complete. Each scene begins with songs and magic. Dialogue between the principal characters ensues. The whole performance of the drama is interspersed in this manner with songs and dance. Today, *jikey* is on the point of extinction.

Scene from a *jikey* performance in Kedah, Malaysia.
(Photo by Ghulam-Sarwar Yousof)

Jin

The word *jin*, also spelt *jinn*, originally from Arabic, referred to spirits in general. This broad definition is, to some extent, maintained in Southeast Asian Muslim communities, so that *jin* are often thought identical to *hantu*, both malevolent and beneficent, belonging to many categories. Sanction for the existence of *jin* is provided in the Holy Quran and the fusion with the concept of hantu arises from syncretism with pre-Islamic belief systems. This often allows the terms *jin* and *hantu* to be used interchangeably. This total identification between the two categories of invisible entities leads to a twofold division suggesting that some *jin* have submitted to Islam and are therefore named *jin Islam* while others have remained infidels, *jin kafir*.

Jin are usually conceived of as being physically huge as well as ugly and frightening in appearance. In keeping with Islamic tradition, they are believed to have been created out of fire and are thus depicted in theatre as red. Their ferocious appearance is heightened with protruding teeth and long hair. *Jin* are believed capable of assuming diverse shapes, including those of animals and human beings. In behaviour, they are, as a rule, presented as crude. They live on animals, insects and even on human beings. This does not preclude the possibility of noble behaviour.

Jin play a significant role in the activities of a traditional healer (*bomoh*), at times as personifications of diseases, at other times as his helpers, in keeping with the view that they can be captured and used by those who possess special magical powers. *Jin* also appear as spirits or even as giants or ogres (*gergasi* or *raksasa*) in theatre rituals connected with traditional genres as well as characters. The best known of these figures is *Jin Afrit*.

A shadow play puppet
in *wayang kulit*
Kelantan, Malaysia.
(Photo by Ghulam-
Sarwar Yousof)

Jin Afrit

The character of *Jin Afrit* or Raja Jin (King of the Genies) as that of the antagonist or evil figure appears in *bangsawan* performances. He is usually represented as large-built, coarse and evil. However, no matter how physically overwhelming and loud a *jin* character may be, as a symbol of evil he never wins in a battle against the noble hero (*orang muda*). The actor performing the *jin* role is usually made up to look awe-inspiring, with a moustache, beard and fangs in addition to a painted face and ruffled hair. *Jin* generally appear in stories derived from Middle Eastern sources such as the *One Thousand and One Nights* or in Indian-Muslim tales such as *Bunga Bakawali*.

Joget Gamelan

Joget gamelan is a dance form originally developed in Pahang and performed to the accompaniment of gamelan Melayu. *Joget gamelan* is done exclusively by female dancers who use fans and scarves as stage properties. Dances begin and end with the traditional salutation (*sembah*) gesture. *Joget gamelan* had a large repertoire of dance but most have not been performed following the loss of court patronage in the early 20th century. Dances are based on plots taken from the Javanese Panji romance, Malay epics as well as folk tales. One of the best known is the *Timan Burung* dance, depicting the situation of a princess trying to catch a bird.

K

Kayangan

In Malay mythology and traditional literature, particularly romances, *kayangan* or *keyangan* is the sky country, the home of the gods (*dewa*) and occasionally ogres (*raksasa*). Instead of a single heaven or upper world, however, there appear to be several, possibly representing different levels or parts. The term *kayangan*, in all probability, is from Javanese mythology and connected with the word *hyang* for god. However, it has parallels with the concepts found in Hindu mythology, and is to some extent equivalent to the term *swarga*. At times, the name of *kayangan* includes that of a deity from the Hindu pantheon, as in *Indra Kayangan/Indraloka*. Thus, it appears that *kayangan* is the general home of the gods, while various *loka* are the homes of particular deities.

Kekitaan

This is a term, from the basic personal pronoun *kita* meaning "I" or "we". Best translated as "our-ness", it implies a sense of belonging. As far as an individual and others of the same group or community are concerned, the connection may be seen in terms of *"orang kita"* (insiders) as opposed to *"dia/depa/demo"* (outsiders). Seen in terms of local values, *kekitaan* extends to appropriating a whole range of concepts, ideas as well as elements. Islam has become *agama kita*, a Malay rather than a world religion. Extended beyond the Malay sphere, it is *ugama orang Melayu* or *ugama orang Arab*, a notion that only these two peoples—Arabs and Malays—are proper Muslims, while others are peripheral, alien, "different" and in some ways inferior. Finally, *kekitaan* may be seen as a sudden urge to accept as Malay something previously ignored, when it brings material or intangible benefits or prestige. Recent examples include certain Indonesian arts forms such as *kuda kepang* and *barongan*, both Javanese, which the Malays tried to appropriate, and *mak yong*, the Kelantanese theatre form, languishing for a century, which has become a status symbol for a small segment of Malays due to recognition given to it by UNESCO. This has come about despite certain inherent conflicts and contradictions, such as the presence of animistic elements that, though needing to be resolved, are conveniently overlooked.

Keramat

Keramat is an Arabic word meaning saintly, miraculous as well as referring to persons who work miracles through their saintliness or holiness. A broader application of the term is used to refer to long deceased saints (*Dato' Keramat*), healers or wonder workers, kings and princes or princesses, such as Puteri Sa'adong of Kelantan or Mahsuri of Langkawi islands, as well as to certain living individuals who have magic power (*sakti*). The graves of such persons are also considered sacred places (*tempat keramat*). Such places are approached by the average person seeking relief from personal problems or to have their wishes fulfilled following the making of vows (*niat*) and the promise of offerings such as yellow rice (*pulut kunyit*) or fruits. Such practices are not very common these days.

Keris

The *keris* is a Javanese asymmetrical dagger most strongly associated with the culture of Indonesia or Javanese culture in other Southeast Asian countries including Malaysia, Thailand, Brunei and Singapore. Although it is believed to be connected with the Dongs'on culture which flourished in Vietnam around 300 BC, the origins of the *keris* in its present form are traced back to the island of Java and more precisely to the 15th century Javanese kingdom of Majapahit. The *keris* is famous for its distinctive wavy blade, although many have straight blades. It can be divided into three parts: the blade (*bilah*) which may be straight or have several waves in it, the hilt (*hulu*) and the sheath (*warangka*). These parts of the *keris* are objects of art. The hulu in particular is often carved in meticulous detail from rare types of wood or ivory, with precious stone embedded into it.

Both as a weapon and spiritual object, *keris* are often considered to have an essence or presence (*semangat*) to the extent of having magical powers. Thus, they are used not only for display but also as talismans. In Javanese culture, *keris* have always played, and some extent still continue to play, an important role in ritual and ceremonies, particularly those associated with the court, but also with the *bomoh* and the puppeteer (*dalang*); they may be seen in coronation as well as wedding ceremonies throughout the region.

Legendary *keris* that possess supernatural power and extraordinary ability are mentioned in *Hikayat* literature, traditional Indonesian histories (*babad*) and so on. One such story connects the *keris* named Taming Sari with the Malay hero Hang Tuah. In many parts of Indonesia, the *keris* with a long and straight blade was the choice weapon for execution. The condemned person knelt before the executioner, who thrust the blade through the shoulder piercing the heart. In Malay legends, this method of execution was known as *salang*, the best example of such execution being that of Mahsuri on the island of Langkawi.

Since Malaysia's independence, the *keris* has become something of a symbol of Malay nationalism.

Keris Taming Sari

Taming Sari ("flower shield") is one of the most well-known *keris* in Malay literature, said to be so skillfully crafted that anyone wielding it was unbeatable. In some versions of the legend, the weapon would grant its user physical invulnerability. The events behind the legend are said to have taken place took place sometime towards the end of the Majapahit Empire and the rise of the Malacca Sultanate. According to *Sejarah Melayu*, the *keris* was made by a Javanese expert and first used by the champion of Majapahit, a warrior named *Taming Sari*. He was defeated in a duel to the death by the Malay warrior Hang Tuah, after which the king of Majapahit presented the weapon to the victor. The *keris* also features in the story of Hang Tuah's final battle with his Hang Jebat who was stabbed by Hang Tuah with *Taming Sari*, and died. Malay legend maintains that *Taming Sari* is still around, and that Hang Tuah would one day return to repossess it.

Artist impression of the *Keris Taming Sari*.
(Sketch by Fiona Wong)

Kesultanan Melaka

The Melaka sultanate was the first and oldest sultanate in Malaysia. It was founded in about 1399 and came to an end with the invasion of the Portuguese in 1511. The kingdom was founded by someone named Parameswara who hailed from Palembang in Sumatra. He and others were forced to leave Palembang due to their political opposition to the power of the Srivijaya empire and conflict between Srivijaya and the Java-based Majapahit empire. Parameswara arrived in Singapore where, following the overthrow of the then ruler, Sang Ranjuna Tapa, he became ruler. Parameswara was in turn overthrown by Sang Ranjuna with the assistance of the Siamese.

Travelling north with a handful of followers, Parameswara reached Melaka where he established a new sultanate in 1399; he ruled until 1414. Melaka gained recognition from the Chinese, with Parameswara sending tribute to the Ming emperor, and it became an important trading centre. Particularly important for Melaka was the visit of the Chinese Admiral, Cheng Ho, in 1409. Parameswara was succeeded by seven rulers before the sultanate was over thrown by the Portuguese.

The institute of Sultanate was first formulated in Melaka and, basically, some of the royal customs and practices then developed, and continue in to this day in Malaysian sultanates. One of the basic principles was that of the Sultan's daulat. The officers of the palace included the *bendahari, perdana menteri, temenggung, laksmana, hulubalang besar* and *syahbandar*. This organizational system continued to be used in subsequent Malay sultanates.

Ketupat

Ketupat are square or polygonal packets of cooked glutinous rice, generally served during Hari Raya with dry-cooked beef (*rendang*). They are made from leaves derived from the coconut (*kelapa*) palm. *Ketupat* can be wrapped in various ways. Well-known wrapping styles include *ketupat pasar, ketupat bawang* and *ketupat satay*. The manner in which these diverse *ketupat* wrappers are woven is essentially the same; the major difference lies in the complexity of the wrappings, particularly the tail (*ekor*) and the head (*kepala*). Of the three types already named, *ketupat bawang* is most popularly used during Hari Raya Puasa. The *ketupat* wrappers are half-filled with uncooked rice, to ensure that the rice cooks well and the *ketupat* shell does not burst open. The rice is boiled in the wrappers until cooked. The *ketupat* are cut open and served with the wrappers on.

Ketupat, wrapped glutinous rice.
(Photo by Ghulam-Sarwar)

Khalwat

Khalwat, from the word *khilvat* which, in the mystical (Sufi) tradition of Islam, means a spiritual retreat characterized by silence, solitude, fasting or abstinence, meditation and other exercises intended to develop devotion and increase capacity for divine love. As ritual practice, *khalwat* may also be identified with the old Malay word *tapa* from the Sanskrit or solitary seclusion as practiced by Hindu ascetics. Various types of *tapa* are mentioned in traditional literature.

In the context of contemporary Malaysia, however, the word *khalwat* has gained a particular and peculiar meaning with reference to unmarried Malay couples or a pair of individuals married but not to each other found in close proximity in secluded or isolated places, be they in the midst of nature such as gardens, in apartments and houses, in hotel rooms or even in parked vehicles. If discovered in such a situation, they are likely to be apprehended and charged for having committed sexual misdemeanour (*khalwat*) by religious officials in a *Syariah* court.

L

Latah

Latah, a peculiarly Malay phenomenon, is usually described as a paroxysmal neurosis. The word is used both for the disease as well as the person affected. There are many views regarding its possible causes, with the majority of sufferers being adult women. *Latah* commonly react in unexpected, startling, even abnormal ways when provoked by some unexpected incident which may in itself be quite trivial. For instance, if someone close by drops something on the floor, if some sudden noise is heard, if a cat screams, or even at the unexpectedly touch by someone. A *latah* reacts in an uncontrollable manner, often mimicking others with some physical action or movement. In addition, the incident may prompt the *latah* to become uncontrollable, to repeatedly utter a nonsensical word or phrase usually trivial or, more likely, obscene. Under normal circumstances, *latah* sufferers do not show any signs of abnormal behaviour or give any indication of their being in any way different from others in their company.

Langkasuka

Langkasuka was an ancient kingdom located in the northern Malay Peninsula. Tradition has it that it was founded in Kedah in the 1st or 2nd century. Its precise location and geographical extent remain unknown. The fact that it is linked with Kedah suggests that it may in fact have been the entity whose remains may still be seen in Bujang Valley. Evidence suggests that Langkasuka was inhabited mostly by Khmer peoples who were ruled by Hindu kings. It adopted Buddhism and a south Indian system of writing.

There is very little historical information regarding Langkasuka. Chinese records over several dynasties from the Liang Dynasty (c. 500 AD) to the Ming Dynasty (1368-1544) give different names for the kingdom. It established relations with China in 515 and sent further embassies in 523, 531 and 568. The name Langkasuka also appears in Malay and Javanese chronicles. Tamil sources name "Ilangasoka" as one of Rajendra Chola's conquests in his expedition against the Srivijaya empire. In the 12th century, the kingdom was a tributary to the Srivijaya empire. Langkasuka appears to have come to an end around the 15th century, leaving no significant trace of any kind. There is a view that it later moved to or was succeeded either by Ligor or Patani, both in southern Thailand today.

Although the known facts and possibilities, given the early dates, make it almost impossible for Langkasuka to be regarded as a Malay kingdom, this has not discouraged Malay imagination from regarding it as one and even as a sign of their ancient civilization. This view may have come about through the yet unproven and so assumed connections between Langkasuka and Patani, perhaps one of the greatest cities in the 17th century, as indicated by *Hikayat Patani*.

Assumed location of the ancient Langkasuka kingdom on the Malay Peninsula. (Sketch by Fiona Wong)

Loka

Loka is a Sanskrit word meaning heaven or at times even hell. It suggests a particular plane of existence such as that inhabited by a particular deity, hence seen as an equivalent to heaven in *swarga loka* and an equivalent to hell, *naraka loka*. Then, there are specific planes or heavens associated with particular deities. These include *Indra loka* for Indra and, *shurga-loka* for Shiva or Betara Guru. There is also a clear division in the use of *loka* into three main categories equivalent to heaven, earth and hell. The terms *shurga* and *naraka* or *neraka* in Bahasa Melayu have come to be regarded as equivalents of the Islamic concepts of heaven and hell, with the third term, *beranta loka*, being translated as the world of mortals or *dunia*. The term *loka*, with all its extensions, found a place in Malay mythology as well as in classical literature.

M

Madrasah

Madrasah are religious schools which succeeded the village *sekolah pondok*, particularly with the active involvement of Arabs, Indian Muslims and, in Penang, the Jawi Peranakan. In many towns, *madrasah* were established in the 19th century within mosques, on properties owned by wealthy merchants as well as properties endowed for religious purposes, these being known as *wakaf* properties. Even following the development of proper religious schools, *madrasah* continue to exist in many places in Malaysia, often within the compounds of mosques, playing the same functions as before.

Mahameru

Literally "the great Meru" in Sanskrit, in Hindu and Buddhist mythology, *Meru* or *Mahameru* is not an actual mountain and the name is applied in general to the whole range of the Himalayas or, more particularly, to Mount Kailasa, the source of the great rivers, the Indus and Brahmaputra, as well as close to the source of the Ganges, India's sacred river. In both Hinduism and Buddhism, *Mahameru* is regarded as the home of the gods and thus the centre of the universe. In Indonesia, some of the loftier peaks such as the Sumeru in Java, the summit which bears the name *Mahameru*, and the Merapi in Sumatra are identified with Meru. Malay mythology also retains the connection of a mountain named *Mahameru* or *Mahabiru* with the gods, while Malay legends as recorded in the *Malay Annals* associate Sumeru with the coming of the first kings.

Main Puteri

Main Puteri is a form of shaman dance active mainly in Kelantan, with roots in animism. It deals with illnesses due to the weakening or loss of a person's vital substance (*semangat*), possession by disease-bearing spirits (*hantu* or *jembalang*) or by something called angin. This is an immense attraction for a particular type of performing art such as *joget*, or identification with a *mak yong* character.

When illness is due to weakening or loss of *semangat*, *main puteri* is staged to bring about a strengthening or recovery return of the vital substance. On the other hand, when a patient is becomes ill due to spirit possession, the offending spirit has to be driven out through a performance. Performances, lasting one or more nights, usually take place following the late night (*isya*) prayer in a patient's house or in a simple temporary stage (*bangsal*) built on the floor. The principal functionaries are the shaman (*tok puteri*), who may be a man or a woman, and an interrogator (*tok minduk*). They are accompanied by several musicians who play a three-stringed spiked fiddle (*rebab*), a pair of bossed gongs (*tetawak*) and a pair of double-headed barrel drums (*gendang*). Additional instruments may at times be used. The rebab player is the chief musician and also acts as the interrogator (*tok minduk*).

In performances involving possession, spirits are summoned and negotiations take place with them. The *tok puteri* acts as a vehicle or placing for spirits as they appear, descending into himself through his trance. The *tok minduk* interrogates them. When the particular spirit responsible for the illness is identified, it is persuaded to leave the patient. The spirit is obliged to accept the offerings and to depart, thus bringing relief to the patient. Offerings are promised given to all spirits who appear and even to those who do not, particularly in more elaborate performances.

In the treatment of *angin*-related problems, a patient has to be directly involved. For instance, when a patient is obsessed with a *mak yong* character, *main puteri* is done in combination with *mak yong*. The patient assumes the role of that particular character even without any previous experience as a performer. The patient is assisted by an experienced *mak yong* artist. Such performances involve emotional release to effect a cure.

Shaman and patient in a *main puteri* performance in Kelantan, Malaysia.
(Photo by Ghulam-Sarwar Yousof)

Mak Inang

Mak Inang is a traditional Malay dance that originated from the time of Malacca Sultanate. The dance is accompanied by a unique music which is believed to have been composed by the order of Sultan Mahmud Shah of Malacca.

In the past, both song and dance were taught to the dancers and singers (*inang*) of the palace for them to perform during royal functions. The dance's movements and its music are so graceful and have all the qualities for court performances. Nowadays, the dance—better known by its modern name as *Inang*—is usually performed during social functions such as wedding receptions.

Mak Yong

Mak yong is a dance-theatre form principally performed in southern Thailand and Kelantan. Rural myths and legends suggest that *mak yong* had supernatural origins.

Basic elements in a performance include dialogue, acting, dances as well as vocal and instrumental music. Several variant styles of folk *mak yong* have been known over the 60 or 70 years. An urban style was developed in Kuala Lumpur in the early 1970s in an attempt to revitalize and modernise the genre, with the establishment of the Seri Temenggung Group in Kelantan. Overall, few active performers remain today, with groups dying out and no real support for the genre. This is the case even though *mak yong* was officially recognised by UNESCO as an item of the Oral and Intangible Heritage of Humanity in 2005.

The traditional dramatic repertoire of *mak yong* consists of 12 plays, the most important of these being *Dewa Muda*. The most important of these, apart from *Dewa Muda*, are *Dewa Pechil*, *Anak Raja Gondang* and *Raja Tangkai Hati*. All stories deal with the adventures of gods (*dewa*) or mythical princes. A troupe of artists may consist of around 15 performers, including musicians.

The basic orchestra consists of three-stringed *rebab*, a pair of double-headed drums (*gendang*) and a pair of gongs (*tetawak*). Additional instruments including, the double-reed oboe (*serunai*) and inverted gongs (*canang*), may be used in certain musical pieces, numbering around 30, but many of them no longer in use today.

Dances in *mak yong*, apart from the elaborate opening piece, *mengadap rebab*, show little variety. Those done by female artists are basically slow and circular with musical, vocal and choric accompaniment. Male performers have stylised dances incorporating various steps and turns which end up in poses.

In addition to four musicians, a group may include approximately seven or eight actresses-cum-dancers and two to four actors, so that a troupe may be made up of around 15 persons, including the musicians. Female performers play the leading male (*pak yong*) role as well as the leading female roles (*mak yong*). Men play the comic (*peran*) roles and a host of other supporting parts including the gods (*dewa*), ogres (*bota/raksasa*), as well as animals and birds. Women play the roles of palace servants (*inang, dayang*) as well as dancers. When not actually involved in the action, they serve as members of chorus (*jung dondang*).

Few multi-functional stage or hand properties are used: for the *pak yong*, a few strands of bamboo tied together into a wand (*rotan berai*) as well as a *keris*; and wooden swords (*golok*) for the *peran* actors. Similarly, simple properties may be used by other performers. All basic information related to time and place regarding action is enshrined within the dialogue and song-texts. The longer songs are accompanied by circular dances serving a multitude of purposes including that of scene-changing.

Performances take one to three nights, commencing at about 9:00 p.m. and ending around midnight. They are preceded by theatre opening rituals. These are followed by a musical prelude with the final piece bringing in the actresses onto the stage for the *mengadap rebab* dance and song. This leads on into several musical pieces sung to the accompaniment of dances performed either in groups or solo. This entire sequence prepares for the story through the appearance of a pair of comic figures (*peran*) before the *pak yong*. With the self-introduction of the *pak yong* as a character, the plot of the selected play begins to unravel. The story is continued during the second and subsequent nights, and upon its conclusion on the final night, the theatre is ritually closed.

Scene from a *mak yong* performance
in Kelantan, Malaysia.
(Photo by Ghulam-Sarwar Yousof)

Mambang

Mambang were minor divinities popularly identified with the tints of the sunset-glow some of which are thought malevolent. Among these, *mambang kuning* are thought to be the cause of jaundice. In some localities, the *mambang* are regarded as birth spirits. The name *mambang* is also given to the four great spirits of the sea.

Mantera and Jampi

Mantera or *mentera* (*mantra* in Sanskrit), in its original Hindu sense, is a sacred word, syllable or phrase, usually uttered by Brahmins, yogis or magicians, as well as by almost anyone, in the Sanskrit language. The word continues in Malay culture, with alternative terms such as *jampi* or *jampi serapah*, with identical meaning. *Mantera* take the form of incantations or as charms in a number of different situations and serve many purposes. In rural Malay communities, apart from private uses by individuals, *mantera* also play a role in a wide range of rituals and magical practices. They are used in a whole range of ceremonies involving magic—from building a house, fishing, farming, healing or staging a performance. All of these involve a traditional *bomoh* since contact between man and invisible entities takes place.

With the conversion of the Malays into Islam, animistic as well as Hindu elements were reduced but not totally eliminated. Thus, while invocations texts or *mantera* continue in folk practices in their traditional forms, even with the inclusion of certain Sanskrit texts in attempts to deal with animistic or Hindu mythic figures, they are often presented in combination with Islamic religious formulae. The following is an example from a m*ak yong* performance:

> I wish to send my greetings to the Guardian of the village. Hey Sang Bima, Guardian of the Village, I wish to make a request to you and your companions, the Guardians of the Village. I ask you not to come and sue or prosecute (i.e. attack), do any unwarranted harm to the seven troupe members and the five bridegrooms, together with the Pak Yong, Mak Yong, the elder Peran, the younger Peran, the children young and old, the young and aged in the theatre and outside the theatre, this theater of Inu, the acting area of Semar, the theatre of Turas. I have come here to this village, your place, to put on a performance representing the gods. I wish to ask your members without intending to leave out anyone (though I make this request) without mentioning all their names.
>
> [Translated from Malay by Ghulam-Sarwar Yusof]

Martabat

Martabat, from Arabic, means rung of a ladder a step or grade in rank. Often pronounced in the Malay language, it implies prestige and respect resulting from good reputation or achievements. As a verb, it also means "to place on a pedestal". In a feudal system, it is expected that grades or degree indicating a person's position in society would be important or play a role in everyday situations. This was the case in traditional Malay society. With modernization, it has become broader in its everyday usage, referring to the rise of prestige through the awarding of titles or medals (*darjah kebesaran*) by the king (*Yang Dipertuan Agong*) rulers of states as well as governors.

Today, the word has come into wider usage in the Malay language. It does not only refer to degree or ranks of persons, but also to other things. An interesting usage was when the National Theatre (*Istana Budaya*) decided to take the *mak yong* theatre from the village and place it on its stage. It was declared that the intention was to *memartabat-kan* mak yong, place it "on the world stage", to raise it from a village folk theatre form to something parallel or even equivalent to Broadway musicals. In principle, the word *martabat* and the concept behind it can, therefore, be applied in this manner, apart from persons, to virtually anything that could, in theory, be elevated, given greater prominence or prestige.

Maruah

The word *maruah* comes from the Arabic word *muruwah*. It may be defined as a sense of self-pride, boldness, honour, reverence for ancestors, respect for other members of a tribe or community, and so on. Overall, it implies adherence to a chivalric code of conduct within the tribe or community, especially during the pre-Islamic Jahiliyya period, the so-called Age of Ignorance. While some of these applications of tribal pride may have been borrowed by the Malays from the Arabs, in the local context, *maruah* may be seen, in a variant version, in adherence and loyalty to the community, or a segment of it, especially when it faces or is seen to face challenges from another. In a modern sense, such adherence shifts towards institutions such as race-based political parties or organizations. While this is the general situation, *maruah* may also be seen to operate on a more personal level.

Masjid Kampung Laut

Masjid Kampung Laut in Kelantan is the oldest existing mosque in Malaysia. Named after the village in which it was originally built, there are several stories connected with its origins. One such tale maintains that the mosque was built by Raja Imam, a Javanese native who came to the Malay Peninsula with three of his brothers. Another story has it that the mosque was built by an unnamed Islamic scholar from Java. In both instances, there is agreement that the mosque was constructed in the 18th century, before the reign of Long Yunus (1762-1795), Kelantan's first ruler.

Masjid Kampung Laut was built using *cengal batu* wood, with only wooden nails in its construction. The design of the mosque, with its three-tiered roof and a square prayer hall, is the same as that of Masjid Agung Demak in Central Java. This is in turn believed to have been based on identical designs in Kerala, South India, reflecting influences from Hindu architecture. Various alterations took place to *Masjid Kampung Laut* up to the reign of Sultan Mansur (1890-1900). At the end of the 1960s, Kampung Laut was flooded, causing part of the mosque to sink into the Kelantan River. Efforts to rebuild it in its original form took place in 1968 and the completed mosque was moved to the Islamic Higher Education Foundation (*Yayasan Pengajian Tinggi Islam Kelantan*) in Nilam Puri.

Masjid Kampung Laut in Nilam Puri, Kelantan, Malaysia.
(Photo by Ghulam-Sarwar Yousof)

Masuk Jawi

Masuk jawi is a termed used instead of *bersunat* or *berkhatan* to refer to the act of getting circumcised. In Islam, circumcision for boys is not an absolute requirement, hence the local name *sunnat*, which generally describes an act that is not compulsory but meritorious. Circumcision of boys usually takes place between the age of 10 and 12 and in the traditional rural context, the ceremony is normally done by a male person known as the *tukang sunat* or respectfully as *tok mudin*.

On the day for the circumcision, a feast is given in the morning. The boy to be circumcised will have his head completely shaved. The items required for the ceremony include a banana stem (*batang pisang*), a piece of unstitched *sarung* to be worn by the boy during the circumcision, a betel box complete with all its accessories, a suitable knife for the circumcision, and a sum of 1.25 ringgit as an offering, usually given to the *tok mudin* in addition to his professional fee.

Before the ceremony, the boy bathes at the nearby well or river, following which water from a gourd is used to give him a bath. The boy chews some betel leaves, something that indicates his bravery or heroism; to chew to make him "brave". The boy then sits on the banana stem and the Tok Mudin proceeds with the ceremony and bandages the wound before the boy is taken to a resting area. Neighbours customarily visit the circumcised boy and his parents.

Mass circumcision ceremonies, occasionally seen in villages, may involve a large group of boys. These are done of the basis of co-operation (*gotong royong*) between the families involved, with all costs involved shared by them. Such ceremonies are often timed to coincide with that of another important event in the life of a boy, the completion of the reading of the Holy Quran (*khatam al-Quran*).

Masuk Melayu

There is a strange phenomenon existing only among the Malays. This is the total identification of one's race with religion. This is different from the concept of national religion as seen, for instance, in Nepal, regarded as the world's only Hindu state, and perhaps some of the other Muslim countries.

In the case of Malaysia, due to the identification of the Malays as a race with Islam and the widespread inability to see the difference between race and religion, a person who converts from another religion into Islam is said to *masuk Melayu* (become Malay) rather than the more accurate *masuk Islam* (to become a Muslim). The immediate implications of this identification of race with religion are clear, at least, in terms of certain benefits that go to the Malays, in theory also to the new Malays. Rightly or wrong, there are numerous non-Malays who are said to *masuk Melayu* upon converting to Islam, literally changing their race, logically an impossibility.

Although in theory such conversions allow the *saudara baru* (new relations) all the rights and privileges of the Malays, in reality, it presents a rather complicated picture. It appears that such rights and privileges are accorded based upon other often indefinable criteria: the most powerful of these being political leanings and party affiliation.

Mek Mulong

Mek mulong is a dance-theatre form active only in the village of Wang Tepus in Kedah. The name *mek mulong* appears to have from two words, *mek*, meaning girl or lady and *mulung*, believed to be the name of a forest in which the genre first started.

The traditional *mek mulong* repertoire consisted of 12 stories, most of them mythical or legendary in character with divine or superhuman heroes. Of these, few are still staged. The principal roles in *mek mulong* consist of the following: the principal male role (*pak mulung*), representing the hero (*wira*) of a story; *mek mulung*, the principal female role, representing the heroine (*wirawati*); and *peran* or *pengasuh* the male comic attendants of whom there generally are four in a performance; and finally, the *inang* or *inang pengasuh*, female attendants serving the queen or princess. Several secondary roles such as opponents (*musuh*) of the hero, may also be used, depending upon the story performed. They may be human enemies or supernatural beings such as giants (*gergasi*). Although some change is being introduced into *mek mulong* in this respect, on the whole, the traditional practice of using male performers for all roles continues.

Only the bare minimum equipment is required for a *mek mulong* performance. The orchestra consists of a double-reed oboe (*serunai*), four frame drums (*rebana*) in two pairs of different sizes, a gong, a pair of cymbals (*mong*) and five pieces of bamboo clappers (*cerek*). The *raja* character uses a prop consisting of bamboo split into seven strands (*rotan tujuh*) or a carved stick (*kayu lorek*) approximately a foot and a half in length. This serves as a weapon as well as a scepter. In fact, sometimes the *kayu lorek* consists of a bundle of seven coconut leaf stems. The clown (*awang pengasuh*) characters use wooden knives (*parang*) believed to possess magical power (*sakti*). Costumes in *mek mulong* are basic, except for that of the *raja*. He wears a traditional long-sleeved Malay-style shirt (*baju Melayu*), a pair of pants and over them a short sarong (*sampin*) reaching down to the knees. A headgear (*tanjak*) completes his costume. The principal female characters (*puteri*) wear normal village clothes, usually consisting of a *sarong* and *kebaya*. The clown actors (*peran*) are also dressed in everyday clothing, consisting of a shirt and a sarong. They are sometimes bare-topped. The most interesting and important feature of the clown costumes are the wooden masks, carved and painted in keeping with their roles. The principal clown (*ketua peran*) wears a black mask whereas the others use red ones.

Mek mulong performances are divided into two categories: normal ones and those intended to salute the ancestors or teachers (*sembah guru*). The latter type, done annually, are spiritually more significant and elaborate.

Murka

The word *murka*, deriving from Sanskrit, means wrath or anger, particularly that of God or a ruler. In general, Malaysian history, as well as traditional literature, demonstrate many situations where the anger of a ruler or king results in severe punishment such as imprisonment, banishment from one of the Malay States or death sentence for acts of disobedience or disloyalty, generally referred to as *derhaka*. The classic cases are those of the two Malacca heroes Hang Tuah and Hang Jebat.

N

Nasi

Nasi, or cooked white rice, is the staple food of Southeast Asian communities. However, among the Malays, there exist various other types of nasi, including *nasi ambeng, nasi dagang, nasi himpit, nasi lemak* and *nasi belauk,* cooked differently from the normal boiled or steamed rice, the differences coming about from additional ingredients. *Nasi ambeng* includes red beans, long beans, potatoes, soya bean cakes (*tempe*) and toasted chicken (*ayam*) and cooked with a layer of banana leaves. *Nasi ambeng* came from Demak in Java, where it has been served various traditional ceremonies. Participants in such ceremonies are also given packed *nasi ambeng* to take home with them, so that those not actually present can also enjoy the rice and receive blessings (*berkat*).

Nasi dagang is plain or glutinous rice (*pulut*) which is red in colour, mixed with coconut juice (*santan*), red onions, and ginger and cooked with meat, including fish, chicken, or beef meat. It is eaten with cucumber pickles (*acar*). *Nasi dagang* is usually served for breakfast; in Kelantan and Terengganu, where it is popular, *nasi dagang* may also be served during the Hari Raya festival.

Nasi lemak is rice cooked with coconut juice, ginger, aniseed, fennel and salt. It is quite commonly encountered in restaurants and eating stalls (*gerai makan*) and packed in paper with a layering of banana leaves. *Nasi lemak,* eaten as a snack at any time of the day or as a full meal, is also served like normal rice in up-market restaurants. *Nasi lemak* usually comes with sauce (*sambal*) made

A serving of nasi *lemak* with boiled egg, cucumber, peanuts, anchovies and *sambal.*
(Photo by Fiona Wong)

from anchovies (*ikan bilis*), part of a boiled egg, some vegetable, a slice of cucumber and fried ground nuts.

Other varieties of rice include rice cooked with oil or ghee (*nasi minyak*), and *nasi beriani*, rice cooked with chicken, beef or mutton. These dishes and yet others, introduced into Malaysia from India, Pakistan, the Middle East and Iran, have become popular among members of all communities in the country.

Neraka

The word *neraka*, from the Sanskrit *naraka*, is equivalent to the idea of hell in the Judaeo-Christian as well as Islamic traditions. It represents a place or places said to number 28 where sinners are tormented after death. The Malay certainly got the term *neraka* if not the actual description and context from Hinduism. With the coming of Islam, Islamic ideas of hell and heaven superseded animistic as well as Hindu-Buddhist beliefs among the Malays. While still retaining South Asian terms, for both heaven (*swarga* tuned into *shorga* or *shurga*) and hell, as in the case of other mythological terms in general they now accept standard Islamic concepts of both.

Nobat

The word *nobat* derives from the Persian *nau-bah* or *nau-bat*, meaning nine items or, more particularly, a band or orchestra of nine voices. The *nobat* orchestra was already a tradition in the palaces of the Middle East, whence it spread to Turkey, India and Southeast Asia with the spread of Islam. As far as Southeast Asia is concerned, tradition has it that the first *nobat* orchestra was introduced into Pasai in the 13th century, when its ruler was installed following the introduction of Islam. Then a son-in-law of the queen, named Tri Sri Buana, was installed as king of Singapore to the beat of the *nobat*. When the Malacca sultanate was set up, the *nobat* became one of the royal institutions of its palace.

Among Malaysian states, the *nobat* orchestra is found only in Kedah, Perak, Selangor and Kelantan. It consists of the big drum (*gendang nobat*); the royal trumpet (*nafiri*); two royal kettledrums (*negara*); two non-royal pipes (*serunai*) and two drums (*gendang*). The conductor completes the ensemble as the ninth item. Of these instruments, *gendang nobat* is the most sacrosanct. The basic instruments used by the four *nobat* orchestras in Malaysia are the same, even if the sizes of the instruments vary. The special instruments are usually wrapped with yellow cloth, yellow being the colour of royalty. The instruments are kept in special *nobat* rooms (*bilik nobat*). In Kedah and Perak, they are stored in dedicated buildings known as *balai nobat*.

In the Indian sub-continent, the big drum, named *tabl*, had special connections with royalty. Used only to announce the doings of the king, it was thus regarded as the highest of the instruments of the *nobat* orchestra. Interestingly, this tradition has continued into the Malay states for the installation (*pertabalan*) of a *raja* or *sultan*.

Historically, the *nobat* ensemble, as part of the royal regalia, is a symbol that explains the concept of *daulat* and connects the rulers with the Malay race (*bangsa*) as well as the traditional social and political structure. The music of the *nobat* accompanies all royal ceremonies, and *nobat* has long been accepted as a symbol of the ruler's status and power. The orchestra can only be played by special musicians called *orang Kalur* or *Kalau*.

O

Orang Bunian

Orang bunian, literally those who make a sound, are invisible beings who make whistling sounds. They may be seen only by those with spiritual sight. In appearance, they resemble human beings, are extremely beautiful and are dressed in clothes of ancient style. *Orang bunian* live far away from human habitation in deep forests or high mountains, but are also said to live within human communities, even sharing houses with human beings. Their social structure is similar to that of human beings, with their own royalty, clans and families. *Orang bunian* possess supernatural powers and persons entering their realm must perform certain rites.

Orang bunian have been known to interact with human beings and provide assistance, in particular, to shamans. Malays believe that marriages can take place between *orang bunian* and human beings and that such unions result in invisible children. Stories are told of men who married *bunian* women and disappeared with them, only to find, upon returning to their native villages, that much time has lapsed, and that their families and acquaintances have all died.

Orang Melayu

There have been several theories and much debate regarding the origins and identity of the *orang Melayu* (Malays). Anthropologists maintain that there were two waves of immigration from Yunnan in southeast China into Southeast Asia. The first wave, known as the early or Proto-Malays, arrived in the Malay Peninsula during the late Stone Age, 8,000 BC to 10,000 BC. These were the aboriginal peoples (*orang asli* or *orang asal*). The second wave was made up of the more advanced Deutero-Malays, who were the ancestors of present-day Malays. Traditionally, in the anthropological sense, the word Malay has never stood alone, but as part of compound Malayo-Polynesian.

A second theory claims that the discovery of skulls in the Niah Caves in Sarawak, dating back to 35,000 BC, proves that the "Malays" came from the island of Borneo and spread in all directions by sea to as far as Madagascar, Taiwan and the Pacific islands.

Another view, connected with the second wave mentioned above but taken a step further, indicates that *orang Melayu* in fact had their first home in Sumatra. The name *Malayu* or *Melayu* refers to a river, Sungai Melayu, on the island of Sumatra and to the territory passing through it. Secondarily, it relates to the inhabitants of that area: hence the term *orang Melayu*. The precise dates for the first sign of the existence of *orang Melayu* and their movement remain unclear but the name appears in records referring to the Srivijaya Empire (7th to 13th centuries) centred on Palembang in Sumatra. The name *Malayu*, has also been associated with a kingdom in Jambi in Sumatra, with the two names Jambi and Srivijaya used interchangeably. The kingdom was founded in the 13th century.

Thus, it is more or less evident that *orang Melayu* arrived in the Malay Peninsula from Sumatra in comparatively recent times. Such movements have continued, with many arrivals involving other races and communities, including the Javanese, Bugis, Minangkabau, Acehnese, Mandailing, and so on as part of the Indonesia diaspora. Although conveniently grouped together as Malays, most of them are in fact ethnically non-Malays. The *orang Melayu* of the Malay Peninsula constitute a part of the diaspora, with significant mixtures from the earliest time of peoples from China,

South Asia, Champa and Thailand, followed in recent centuries by a second wave of immigrants from China, South Asia, the Middle East and even the west. Today, these mixed peoples as well as many others who converted into Islam are referred to as *orang Melayu*. Thus, with the reinvention of history as well as appropriate redefinition, the term *orang Melayu* has been vastly expanded in meaning and implication to apply to a whole range of peoples who are in fact ethically non-Malays, mixed or converts into Islam.

This has been due particularly to the desire to create a majority community in Malaysia, which may be regarded as "Malay" according to the Malaysian constitution and the demands of Malaysian politics. The overall meaning of who may be regarded as an *orang Melayu* is thus arbitrary and often confusing. This is particularly the case when the word *Melayu* is taken together with the term *bumiputera*, which, in a general sort of way, refers to the *orang asli* as well as the indigenous people such as those of Sabah and Sarawak who are not Muslims.

P

Panggung

The word *panggung* refers to any sort of theatre building and is also used to refer to cinema-houses. Performances of all traditional performing arts, such as *mak yong* and *main puteri* as well as *silat*, are done in very simple attap and bamboo structures built on the ground. In recent decades, these have become elevated to allow for greater visibility of the performance by larger audiences. *Wayang kulit* has its own box-like structure, totally enclosed except on the front side which is covered with a length of white muslin; on this the shadows of the puppets are cast. *Bangsawan* performances, in times before the construction of permanent theatres in various towns, were done on temporary elevated stages, with space for costume changes provided behind the painted backdrops.

In all traditional genres, not including the relatively new *bangsawan*, performances are preceded by theatre opening rituals, known as *upacara buka panggung*. Various items of offerings are prepared for several categories of spirits. In some instances, a length of yellow cloth (*kain langat*) is suspended below the roof over the *panggung*, with flowers and certain offering items fixed to it and a coin placed on it. A qualified *bomoh* or ritual specialist conducts the rites through reading various incantations (*mantera*) and makes the offerings to the invisible host. He finally gives the signal for the opening of the theatre, allowing the performance to proceed. The final night of a performance or season ends with a closing ceremony (*upacara tutup panggung*) to thank the spirits.

A theatre (*panggung*) for the shadow play in
Kelantan, Malaysia.
(Photo by Ghulam-Sarwar Yousof)

Pantang Larang

Pantang and *larang* are two words usually taken in popular expression as a single phrase or separately. Their meanings have some degree of overlap, with *pantang* referring to taboos while *larang* to what is forbidden. *Pantang larang* enter into almost every department of activity in traditional Malay society. They are also applicable when it comes to offences prescribed by custom (*adat*) or common law such as adultery or murder. The origins of *pantang* are not always clear and they are thus often attributed to superstition. However, they have been maintained as a matter of customary practice in the hope of preventing misfortune or mishap in situations when one is particularly vulnerable or has to deal with unknown forces.

Pantang lay down what a pregnant woman may or may not do during the seventh month of pregnancy as well as for 44 days after the birth of her child; equally, certain *pantang* also apply to her husband during the same period. In other circumstances, particular *pantang* or taboos apply to the harvest, when a sailor or fisherman is at sea, or when someone enters the jungle to hunt or to collect jungle products. In effect, such taboos or prohibitions apply to many other areas of human activity, including traditional sports such as *silat* or cockfighting; to guide the time when and in what manner these activities are carried out.

Larang indicates what is forbidden or prohibited to a person or a class of persons under certain circumstances. Some of these are indicated in pursuance of particular rules, laws or orders issued by appropriate authorities. One may, for instance, be forbidden to enter a protected area, or wear a particular kind of uniform, such as that used by members of the military. In many cases, *larangan* may be translated to mean "reserved" or private, forbidden to the public or segment of the public. Examples are spaces or pavilions reserved for women (*balai larangan*), forest reserves (*hutan larangan*) and so on. In the case of *larang*, there are no taboos or superstitions indicated as in *pantang*.

Pantun

The *pantun* may be defined as a quatrain, a form of literary expression that developed in the oral tradition. In written form, it first found a place in *Sejarah Melayu* and *Hikayat Hang Tuah*, both dating back to the 15th century.

In its basic form, a *pantun* makes use of alternate rhyming scheme (*abab*) with every line containing between 8 and 12 syllables. The first and second lines sometimes appear completely disconnected in meaning from the third and fourth but there is almost invariably a link which comes through association of ideas, thought, feeling or nuance.

Highly allusive, the *pantun* makes use of traditional symbols, an understanding of which enhances one's appreciation of its subtler meanings and intentions. Most of the symbols come from the natural environment. Sometimes, a *pantun* may consist of a series of interwoven quatrains, in which case it is known as a *pantun berkait*. By far, the favourite theme of the *pantun* is love. *Pantun* appear in many different contexts such as in the *bangsawan* theatre, Malay vocal music and through these forms in other media such as films. An example of a *pantun berkait* used on occasions of betrothal goes as follows:

> Small is my cottage, but it has five shelves
> For roasting the *kerisi* fish;
> Hearken, good people, whilst I inquire of you
> What is the price of our Diamond here?
>
> Your fishing line must be five fathoms long
> If you would catch the *tenggiri* fish;
> Seven *tahils*, a *kati* and five *laksa*,
> That is the price of our Diamond here.

(Skeat, *Malay Magic*, New York, Benjamin Blom, 1972, p. 367)

Pending

Pending are large buckles made of gold, silver or brass attached to cloth belts as decorative items of a formal costume. Apart from the Malays, members of the Baba community, the indigenous or *bumiputera* communities, Thais as well as other nationalities within Southeast Asia also make use of *pending*. During the rule of Cik Siti Wan Kembang in 15th century Kelantan, *pending* became part of the official court dress for women to be used with *sarung* and *kain samping*. *Pending* appear in many different shapes, including circular ones and those shaped like *buah kana* or the human eye. In design, they may be plain or elaborate. They are used by ordinary citizens as part of ceremonial dress or dance costumes. *Pending* used by members of royalty have detailed designs inspired by nature, with precious stones at time embedded into them.

Penghulu

From the word *hulu*, meaning head, *penghulu* is a term that refers to chiefs or headmen of all sorts but in modern usage, more to the head of a village (*kampung*). In other situations, there are the head of the kitchen (*penghulu dapur*), head of the palace (*penghulu istana*), mosque-keeper (*penghulu masjid*), etc. Prophet Muhammad is often referred to as the *penghulu* or head of all Mankind, and as the head of all the Prophets. Other equivalent words are *kepala* (head), *ketua* (chief) and so on. On the whole, these have come in greater usage these days as in *ketua jabatan* (head of department), *ketua menteri* (chief minister), *ketua polis* (chief of police) and so on.

Peri

Peri, properly *pari*, are nymphs derived from Persian mythology. The term is used as parallel or identical to the Sanskrit *bidadari* or *apsara* living in the court of the god Indra. Persian mythology has them as descendants of fallen angels who have been denied paradise until they have done penance. They are exquisite, winged, creatures ranking between angels and evil spirits. They sometimes visit the realm of mortals. Appearing often in Middle Eastern and Persian literature, they arrived in Malay literature as a result of the translation of those works and through Persian or Indo-Muslim stories performed in the *bangsawan* theatre.

Imaginary *pari* character.
(Sketch by Fiona Wong)

Pesta

The word *pesta* is of Portuguese origins. It refers to any festive gathering or entertainment. It is also used in the broader sense of village-, town- or city-fairs. The emphasis has shifted these days to grand gatherings of various sorts, including sports events (*pesta sokan*) and fairs held at regular intervals in various locations or cities, the best-known being the annual Festival of Penang (*Pesta Pulau Pinang*) in which a large range of sub-activities, including cultural shows and games, take place. Numerous stall or mini-shops are built to serve food, while clothing, shoes, accessories, electronic gadgets as well as souvenirs may be picked up at others. The habit of visiting such *pesta* must stand out amongst the most important pastimes of the Malays, to the extent that it can be said that any time is *pesta* time.

Polong

The *polong* is an evil and hideous spirit created from the blood of a murdered person kept in a bottle. It is invoked with magic spells and enslaved by someone for personal use, particularly to harm others. The spirit is fed from blood from owner's fingers to assuage its hunger, as well as to ensure that the spirit remains loyal to its master. People attacked by the *polong* are left with bruises and almost every attack results in blood issuing from the mouth of a victim. In certain instances, when the *polong* is particularly difficult to deal with, a *bomoh* or a preacher (*imam*) from a mosque may be called in to cast it out. It is believed that one of the most effective ways in which to drive away a *polong* is to place seeds of black pepper on certain parts of a victim's body while reciting passages from the Holy Quran. This serves to neutralise a *polong* which may also be forced to reveal the identity of its master.

Puaka

Puaka refers to the spirit of a particular locality which is seen to be then haunted. They are at times identified with earth spirits (*jembalang* and *hantu tanah*) and to them, offerings or sacrifices are given. Homage or reverence paid to such a spirit over time may turn it into a miracle working figure, such as *Dato' Keramat*.

Puja Pantai

Puja Pantai was a ritual in honour of the guardian spirits of the sea that took place in Kelantan and Terengganu once in two or three years when there were indications that the spirits were disturbing farmers or fishermen. It was intended to establish goodwill between those affected and the sea spirits, as well as to seek the cooperation of the spirits in anticipation of misfortune. The ritual, which was officiated by a *bomoh*, took place over three or seven days and nights on or near a beach. During that period, fishermen did not go to sea, but held various forms of entertainment, including *wayang kulit*, *mak yong*, *menora* and *main puteri*, as well as kite flying, for the spirits. These performances took place on specially constructed platforms or theatre structures (*panggung*).

On the final day, an albino buffalo was sacrificed following appropriate preparations. Offerings consisting of parts of its meat, yellow glutinous rice (*pulut kuning*), eggs, betel leaves *and sirih pinang* and *tepung tawar* was placed on the top of a beautifully decorated seven-tiered structure called the *balai*. A *bomoh* read various types of invocations (*jampi serapah*), asking the spirits not to disturb the farmers and fishermen again. The *balai* was then placed on a raft (*rakit*) which was drawn into the sea by sailing boats as an offering to the sea spirits. Following the presentation of the offerings, fishermen were not allowed to go to the sea for three days. This was to allow everything to return to normal with the completion of the ceremonies and the appeasement of the sea spirits. *Puja pantai* has in recent years been banned following the declaration that it is contrary to Islamic practice and sinful (*haram*).

R

Raja/Maharaja

The concepts related to Malay kingship are evident from three words used for the ruler of a state i.e. *Raja, Maharaja* and *Sultan*. These words derive from two distinct cultures. *Raja* and *Maharaja*, originally from the Sanskrit are from South Asia, while the word *Sultan* is derived from the Middle- and Near-East. It may be worth recording that another designation, *Shah*, meaning king, found as part of many royal names as well as, these days, in common Malay names, comes from Parsi.

Historically, in various Southeast Asian and Malay kingdoms where the rulers were named Raja, the practices of coronation (*pertabalan*) particularly included several Hindu rites and practices. In the case of the Malaysian states, the sole example of the use of the term *Raja* to this day is in Perlis. The designation *Maharaja* (Great King or Emperor) continues to be used in the names of King Asoka or the Mughal Emperor Akbar when these rulers are referred to by Malaysian historians.

Among the Malaysian states, the sole instance of such usage was in Johor, where, in consonance with Indian style, the ruler was called Maharaja Abu Bakar (r. 1868-1895), until he adopted the title of *Sultan* in 1885. His wife Fatimah came to be known as the *Maharani*. Interestingly, the same title, *Maharani*, was given by the British to Queen Victoria as "Queen and Empress of India".

Ronggeng

Ronggeng is a social dance involving males and female, with music provided by the viola, accordion, *rebana* and gongs. In the past, *ronggeng* was highly popular during social gatherings such as weddings in both urban and rural areas of the country. The origins of *ronggeng* remain unknown. References to this form of dancing, however, are to be encountered in various old Malay texts such as *Hikayat Hang T*uah and *Tufhat al-N*afis. *Hikayat Hang Tuah* discusses the use of *pantun* singing with the accompaniment of *rebana* drums, gongs and *kecapi*, a plucked stringed instrument. It is possible that *ronggeng* emerged during the 17th or 18th centuries.

During the 1930s and 1940s, groups of *ronggeng* dancers were to be found in various entertainment centres (*taman hiburan*) in many Malayan towns as well as in Singapore. Hostesses danced with guests and received a small fee. *Ronggeng* songs and music were also featured in the stories and extra-turn sections of *bangsawan* performances, as well as Malay films. Through *bangsawan*, *ronggeng* also combined certain Western singing styles and instruments such as flutes, trumpets, trombone, base piano guitar and drums, maracas and tambourines.

These days, the *ronggeng* dance is on the decline, although the music and songs associated with this art form, such as *asli* and *inang* remain popular, and are regularly presented on radio and television.

Artist impression of a
ronggeng dancer. (Sketch
by Fiona Wong)

S

Sakti

In Hinduism, *Shakti*, which also means literally power or energy, refers to supernatural power, or the generative or creative principle of a god personified in the corresponding goddess, such as Durga or Kali as the wife/*shakti* of Shiva. In traditional Malay romances modeled on those from India, *sakti* figures, as a divine power to work miracles, plays a great part in the combats of gods against demons. According to Hindu beliefs, a certain modicum of supernatural power could be acquired by asceticism (*tapa*) and even that this power could be passed on by ascetics to other persons and inanimate objects. This is something that has been carried over into Malay traditional culture. Thus, the power (*sakti*) and the use of talismans (*azimat*) may be encountered in old romances, where the energy of powerful places (*keramat*) may also be seen.

The Malay *bomoh* often claim special powers also known as *sakti*, at times attributing them to gods or invisible forces. These are received directly from the invisible sources, or through a *bomoh*'s own efforts involving meditation or asceticism (*pertapaan*) just as in the case of the heroes of Hindu epics or romances. The magical power resides in the mantera used, in certain instruments or weapons, as well as in the *bomoh* as a person.

Salang

Salang was a form of execution, probably uniquely Malay, in which the victim had to squat down while the executioner stood over him and drove a long, straight-bladed *keris*, known as *keris panjang*, from a certain spot within the collarbone near the neck down far into the heart. The most famous killing or execution of such in Malay legend comes from the story of *Mahsuri*, a woman on the island of Langkawi who was falsely punished for adultery in this manner.

Sambal

In general, the word *sambal* refers to condiments or pickles. There is a wide range of cooked as well as uncooked *sambal* among the Malays, many of them also to be found in various Indonesian communities.

Cooked *sambal* are intended to be served with particular types of food, such as *nasi lemak, ketupat, satay* or just plain rice. Some varieties of cooked *sambal*, such as that made from anchovies (*sambal ikan bilis*) or beef (*sambal daging*) which, dried and properly packed may be kept for long periods of time, have been popular with fishermen, travellers and pilgrims to Mecca.

Uncooked *sambal*, are eaten with rice or other food to add flavouring. The most ubiquitous condiment of this variety is *sambal belacan*. This is a pungent red condiment made from chilies or peppers, onions, shrimp paste, sugar, salt, tamarind and sour fruits such as green lime and unripe mangoes. The name comes from the ingredient *belacan*, which is made from small shrimps or fish fry. Salted, sun dried and allowed to ferment, they are pounded or trodden down in the traditional manner. There are many local types of *sambal* throughout the country, including, the well-known *budu* of Kelantan.

Sandiwara

Sandiwara is a form of Malay-Indonesia theatre developed in the 1950s following the decline of bangsawan. It is generally regarded as the first important style in the development of modern drama due to the fact that, in most instances, *sandiwara* utilised complete scripts compared to *bangsawan* whose performances were developed out of sketchy scenarios. A number of important playwrights, including Shahrom Hussain and Bidin Subari, wrote scripts which are regarded as literary works just like true drama which developed in the following decades.

Developments in *sandiwara* staging also introduced elements relatively nearer to modern theatre. The painted backdrops of *bangsawan* were replaced by built sets; extra turns—the comic sketches, songs and instrumental music appearing between scenes to allow for scene-changes—were eliminated and *sandiwara* techniques, though still romantic or melodramatic, tended to move away from the stereotypical towards naturalism. Perhaps, the most important of all developments in *sandiwara* was the emergence of the modern director. The so-called *sandiwara* period in both Malaysia and Indonesia in fact coincided with the development of the first naturalistic plays in local languages as well as, in the case of Malaysia, in the English language. *Sandiwara* plays continue to be occasionally staged to this day.

Sang Kancil

Sang Kancil is the "hero" of a series of mouse-deer tales, which constitute the most important of all the beast fables of Malaysia and Indonesia. Many other animals, however, are inevitably featured in *Sang Kancil* tales. Motifs or themes from many *Sang Kancil* tales have been traced back to various Indian sources. Two Malay versions of the stories, entitled *Hikayat Pelanduk Janaka* and *Hikayat Sang Kancil* exist. The first, known to scholars since 1736, has been published several times in prose as well as verse. *Hikayat Sang Kancil* was transcribed in the present century. Recent years have seen increasing interest in the tales, with the result that many new collections have made their appearance.

In 1925, the *Sang Kancil* stories provided the inspiration for the development of a shadow play (*wayang kulit*) for children in Indonesia. This is known as *wayang kulit kancil*. A similar form of shadow play, using the *Sang Kancil* story, also developed in Malaysia in the 1970s has died out.

Artist impression of a *kancil*, mouse deer.
(Sketch by Fiona Wong)

Sang Yang Tunggal

The name *Sang Yang Tunggal* means "the One and Only" and it refers to God in the Hindu-Javanese mythology. *Sang Yang Tunggal* has been identified with Shiva, who also has several secondary designations, including *Sang Yang Berdiri Kaki Tunggal* or "the One who stands on a Single Leg". Although it found an important place in Malay traditional literature as well as in folk rituals, there is no evidence that the designation *Sang Yang Tunggal* was used by Malays in their religious practices. However, it still has an important place in the Kelantan shadow play where *Sang Yang Tunggal* is said to be manifested in the figure of Pak Dogol, the genre's principal clown, regarded, in turn, as a version of Semar, the all-important god-clown figure of the Javanese wayang kulit purwa, also believed to be a manifestation of a god.

Sejarah Melayu

Sejarah Melayu is one of the oldest texts in the Malay language and one the most important apart from several *hikayat*. It has been translated into French, German, Dutch Japanese, Tamil and Chinese. There are 29 known versions of the book in various institutions in the world. Of these, several have been studied by scholars, including Abdullah Munshi, W.G. Shellabear, and Richard Winstedt. The original date for the writing of *Sejarah Melayu* remains unknown. It appears that in 1612, Tun Sri Lanang (1565- 1659) oversaw the editorial and compilation process of the work, thus giving us a clear idea of its possible date, as well as its contents. In 1726, Francois Velentijn indicated that the title of the work was *Salatus Salatin* or the *Chronology of Kings*, its principal concern being the line of rulers and their ceremonial. Stamford Raffles renamed the text *Sejarah Melayu (or The Malay Annals)* in 1821 when he got it printed in John Leyden's version. This gave the false impression, which still persists, that the work is in fact a history of the Malay people. Currently, the most popular version in Malaysia is that of William Shellabear (1862–1948).

Overall, apart from events in Melaka, the text of *Sejarah Melayu* does contain some possible indication of Melaka's relations with other territories on the peninsula as well as further afield. These include Pahang, Kelantan, Pasai, Siak Siam, Majapahit and China. Even though its early pages are replete with mythology and even other sections within it cannot be taken as historically accurate, the work is seen as important, since it does provide some insights into what was taking place during the time it covers, in addition to serving as a source of information on the social structure in the times until the fall of Malacca to the Portuguese in 1511. Today, *Sejarah Melayu* is regarded as one of two great Malay texts (*karya agung*), the other being *Hikayat Hang Tuah*.

Sekolah Pondok

Sekolah pondok are village schools with an Islamic curriculum, including the teaching of Arabic language, the Holy Quran, prayers and other subjects connected with the religion. Before the introduction of western education, such schools were usually built in rural areas as well as on outlying areas of towns and cities. The name *sekolah pondok* gradually gave way to the term *madrasah*.

Selampit

Selampit is a form of Malay story telling with theatrical elements active in the state of Perlis as well as on the island of Langkawi off the Kedah coast line. *Selampit* is staged by a single performer without stage properties or musical instruments.

Performances of *selampit* begin with simple theatre-opening rituals (*buka panggung*) involving burning of incense, making of offerings (*kenduri*), the reciting of ritual formulae (*mantera*), and an optional salutation song in which the audience, including denizens of the spirit world, are addressed. The performer both welcomes the audience and apologises in advance for any potential mistakes.

Selampit performances incorporate the development of a plot through rhythmic narration, declamation, chanting or singing techniques. The stories are derived from a repertoire existing principally in the oral tradition. These include *Terung Pipit*, *Malim Deman* and *Si Suton*, which have become classics of Malay traditional literature. The theatrical element in *selampit* consists of the constant transformation of the performer into one or more characters and the use of spoken dramatic texts. Through an evening's performance, lasting perhaps several hours, the single performer assumes by turn the many roles that any selected episodes requires. Costumes changes or masks do not feature in *selampit*.

Selampit performer from
Perlis, Malaysia.
(Photo by Ghulam-Sarwar Yousof)

Semangat

The word *semangat* can be translated as energy or vitality, as spirit or as soul. The first may be seen in terms of physical strength or the desire to do undertake some activity; the second meaning, related indirectly to the first, is used in contexts such as the spirit of nationalism or the spirit of wanting to fight or challenge and so on.

Thirdly, usage of the word *semangat* in certain dialects such as that of Kelantan, has the meaning of "beings of the invisible world", or spirits. It thus becomes a euphemism for *hantu*, when villagers have fear of or reservations in mentioning spirit entities by name. In general then, all spirits are called *semangat*. In a more particular sense, it can be seen in the example of *semangat padi*, the spirit or goddess of rice.

The most important and interesting use of the word *semangat*, however, becomes evident when it is applied to the general concept of soul in broader animistic sense. *Semangat* is then seen as the vital energy or soul substance that is to be found in every entity regarded as living, the lowest of these being those normally regarded as inanimate objects: stones, trees, and metals. Of these, metal objects such as the *keris* are regarded as possessing higher or greater concentrations of *semangat* and this is also the case with other items of royal regalia.

In the case of human beings, a distinction is made between *semangat* and *ruh* or *roh*. *Semangat* is found in greatest concentration in certain parts of the body such as hair and bones. It may be stolen or weakened through black magic, resulting in a loss of physical as well as spiritual vitality. In such instances, specialist healers (*bomoh*) may be called in to assist. Treatment methods may include *belian*, *bagih* or *main puteri*.

Semangat Padi

Semangat padi is literally the energy or spirit of the rice. It is believed that it makes the rice flourish, takes care of the paddy fields, as well as helps in increasing the yield. Hence, the Malays regard *semangat padi* with a measure of awe, even respect. *Upacara semangat padi* is the proper name of the ritual connected with the planting and harvesting of rice. On a fixed day, a *bomoh* will harvest the first sheaves or seeds of rice. A small knife (*tuai*) that can be clasped in one hand is used with the assurance that the energy or spirit of the rice will not go away. The *bomoh* also seeks assurance from the spirits that the seeds will be well taken care of.

When the seeds, having sprouted, are moved to be planted in the actual plot in the paddy field, assurance is once again sought from spirit beings so that the rice-plants are not disturbed in any way. The ritual of *semangat padi* combines Hindu invocations (*mantera*) in Sanskrit and Islamic supplications (*doa selamat*) in Arabic.

Sembah

The term *sembah* refers to obeisance, worship or the act of paying homage; this item also refers to a particular gesture used in such situations. In the *sembah* gesture, the hands are put together with the palms touching each other, as if in prayer, with the finger tips touching. They are then raised in order to salute someone, traditionally at three levels: at the chest, at the chin just below the nose or at the forehead, the position depending upon the status of the person being saluted. In general, the salutation at the forehead is executed when salutation is intended for the king or *raja*. The Malay share the practice of doing *sembah* with many other peoples of the Indian sub-continent as well as their immediate neighbours in Southeast Asia, particularly where Hinduism or Buddhism prevailed in the past and continue do so, as in Myanmar, Thailand or Cambodia. This gesture has also found its way into various local dances and traditional theatre forms such as *mak yong* or *bangsawan*, particularly when the plays are set in royal courts.

Traditionally, the *sembah* is executed in a standing position, but there were variations to this in the past as indicated in classical literature. The gesture originated as an Indian customary practice. In Indian tradition, the gesture is known as *anjali*. In Hinduism, *sembah* positioned at the highest level, at the forehead, or even above the head, indicates worship of the divine in the form of any of the deities. It continues to be used as a means of paying respects to parents, elders and priests. In such instances, body positions may change from standing to bowing, kneeling or even bending low with the forehead touching the floor, particularly in temples or before royalty. Some remnants of this may be seen in Thai Buddhist practices, as well as in Indonesian ceremonial situations. Among the Malays, with the greater awareness of Islam creeping in, the *sembah* gesture is seen less and less, even in ceremonies involving members of royalty as well as in customary practices.

Sembah scene in a *bangsawan* performance.
(Photo by Ghulam-Sarwar Yousof)

Sembah Guru

In traditional theatre genres such as *mak yong* and *wayang kulit*, *sembah guru* is the act of paying homage or respect to one's teacher. Special ritual (*berjamu*) performances, done for this purpose, allow the pupil to legitimately inherit the knowledge as well as skills acquired during the period of training. These conclude with the actual act of *sembah guru* in which the teacher "hands over" such knowledge as well as skills, so that they rightfully belong to the pupil. This allows the new initiate to perform independently, establish his own troupe as well as, in turn, become a guide to others.

Sembah guru (initation) scene of Khatijah binti Awang, a
well known *mak yong* performer in Malaysia.
(Photo by Ghulam-Sarwar Yousof)

Sembahyang

Traditionally, the word *sembahyang* was used from ancient times for prayers, whether done individually or in congregation. Mostly, this word comes from the animistic practice of paying homage (*sembah*) to *hyang*, one or more deities, spirits, of pre-Islamic faiths, particularly animism, as well as to deceased ancestors. Although the word continues to be used in the Malay language, a greater tendency has developed in recent decades to use the Arabic word *salah*, often written in Malay as *solat*. On some signboards and mosques in the country one still sees signboards with the following words: *"Sembahyanglah sebelumanda disembahyangkan"* which may be translated as "Pray before your (dead) body is prayed upon", referring to funeral prayers (*sembahyang janazah*) conducted for the deceased before the burial of the body.

Seri

In Hindu mythology, *Sri* is the wife of Vishnu. She is represented on old monuments as four-armed and, associated specially with the lotus, she is the goddess of fertility. This belief in *Seri* as the fertility goddess was carried over to Indonesia where, known as *Dewi Seri* or *Nyai Seri*, she is the good genius of the rice crop. Among the Malays, the rice spirit is merely called *semangat padi* without any particular name being assigned to her.

Shurga/Sorga

The Malay term *shurga* is from the Sanskrit *Svarga* and the concept behind it is from Hinduism. *Svarga* is a one of seven planes (*loka*) in Hindu cosmology, all located on or above Mount Meru. It is a paradise where the righteous live before their next reincarnation. *Svarga* is presided over by Indra, the chief of the gods (*deva*). Traditional Malay mythology and literature do make references to the idea of *svarga*, morphed into *shurga* or *sorga*. There are particular references to Indra's heaven, in particular, in classical as well as folk literature borrowed from India and translated into Bahasa Melayu. In general, however the concept of heaven in Malay thinking is taken from the concept of *jannah* in Islamic teaching, which also maintains the idea of the seven heavens. Similarly, the Hindu concept of *neraka* or hell has been incorporate into Malay thinking but adapted in terms of the Islamic idea of hell, *jahannam*. The traditional and popular, rather than the strictly Islamic, views of heaven thus represent a combination of animistic ideas, those that came in through Hinduism, and those derived from the Middle East through Islam.

Silat

Silat is the generic name for traditional Malay-Indonesian martial arts; many *silat* forms exist, most of them serving as means of self-defence. Music, usually provided by a small orchestra typically consisting of double-headed barrel drums (*gendang*) and oboes (*serunai*) as well as weapons, in particular the short dagger (*keris*), are used in certain styles. Most *silat* styles consist of combat in pairs. Stylised movements, at times highly ornate and approaching dance, may be used. Religious or mystical elements are not altogether absent and many variant *silat* styles are traced back to or derived from specific Islamic cults or movements. They are handed down in a chain of transmission from some venerable founder. Due to this connection with the supernatural, most *silat* performances or demonstrations commence with invocations and offerings similar to those used in traditional theatre. Many forms of *silat* involve initiation processes and some are characterised by trance.

Artist impression of a *silat* duel. (Sketch by Fiona Wong)

Sirih

Sirih, the betel leaf, is important in traditional Malay culture and customary practices as well as in medicine. In a wedding, for instance, the first step following the agreement to a marriage is the official approach or *meminang*, equivalent to an engagement. Among the gift items (*hantaran*), *sirih* are a priority item. The leaves are decorated with other flowers into a cone-like arrangement known as *sirih junjung*. Placedin a container (*tepak sirih*), this arrangement is borne on the head by a member of the visiting party.

On all important occasions, whenever guests arrive, *sirih*, together with gambir, betel nuts and lime (*kapur*), are served. If negotiations are involved, this act of taking a quid of *sirih* suggests a readiness to begin discussions. Betel leaves are used in appointing of a midwife (*bidan*), as well as in many other rites and ceremonies, including those for opening a theatre (*panggung*). To make one's face more charming (*seri*), special charms (*mantera*) are read over *sirih* and eaten for three consecutive days before sunrise.

In traditional Malay medicine, *sirih* mixed with betel nuts, tumeric and other ingredients are used. Depending upon the illness, the mixture is eaten, applied to the body or spattered from the mouth in the area where the patient sits or lies. It is believed that to be effective, the leaves must be plucked using only the thumb and middle finger of the right hand. The person who does the plucking then has to step backward and to read verses (*salawat*) in honour of Prophet Muhammad.

These days, the eating of *sirih* is no longer common practice in Malay culture although they continue to be used in the preparing herbal medicines.

Songkok

A *songkok* is a traditional untasseled cap made of cloth or velvet. This traditional cap is worn in Malaysia, Indonesia, Brunei, Singapore, southern Philippines and southern Thailand, mostly amongst Muslims. There is no religious value attached to wearing this headgear and in Indonesia, it is commonly also worn by non-Muslims. In Malaysia, the *songkok* is also called *kepiah* or *kopiah*, in common with the skull-cap. This name is also used in southern Philippines. The *songkok* may have had its origins in Indonesia, although there is a possibility that it was introduced from India where variations of the same cap are still in use. These are said to have developed from the Turkish *fez* or *tarbuz*, a tall tasselled hat also seen the Egypt.

The *songkok* has become the national headgear in Indonesia as well as Brunei. When used in formal situations, the *songkok* is black and is usually worn with the full *baju Melayu* set. It is, however, also used with normal pants and shirts. Recent years have seen *songkok* and *baju Melayu* sets appear in a wide range of colours, particularly on occasions such as Hari Raya Puasa. *Songkok* are even made with added borders (*lilitan*) of brocade or silk stitched to the lower edges. The better quality *songkok* are usually unfolded and kept in boxes to be used at the proper time. Foldable *songkok*, which are more easily portable and better suited for daily use, are also readily available.

Songkok, a popular Malay head-gear.
(Photo by Fiona Wong)

Songket

Songket, also at times spelt as *sungkit*, is a kind of weaving that make use of gold thread on a heavy base of silk material. Known since about the 16th century, this art form is practiced in several islands and coastal regions of Southeast Asia and there exist variations in what are known as *Sungkit Sembawa, Sungkit Aceh, Sungkit Palembang* and so on. In Malaysia, *songket* is connected with the states of Kelantan and Terengganu.

Songket material comes in various colours, the commonest being black, dark green and various shades of red, including blood red and mangosteen red. In recent times, the range of colours has expanded to include sky blue, purple, white, and golden yellow, this being the special colour of royalty. Indian motifs were once seen on *songket*, based on the shapes of the lotus or peacock, but these have been subsumed to become less naturalistic. Motifs on *songket* material come principally from nature, with flowers, leaves, fruits and birds being dominant. In general, the garments that result from *songket* material include long women's tunics (*baju kurung*) and wrap-around around skirts (*sarung*) in a set. The patterns are used in several ways to serve as decorations on the entire piece of *songket* material used. They are referred to as scattered flowers (*bunga* or *corak tabur*, or *bunga penuh*) since they fill the whole piece of *songket* used. Other shapes may be used for the top and bottom borders. In the case of the *sarung*, what is known as the *kepala*, or head, in the form of a vertical panel at the centre of the piece, is usually decorated with the bamboo shoot design known as *pucuk rebung* and *lawi ayam*. For the making of upper garments for women, such as *baju kurung*, or blouses, overall floral designs such as those already mentioned or diamond shapes have been in constant vogue. For a *sarung* piece, apart from the *kepala*, less elaborate designs, usually in a series known as *rantai* (chain) are used.

In the past, *songket* was meant for royalty. However, this has changed with clothes made of *kain songket* being used at various levels of society, particularly for use in formal or ceremonial situations such as weddings, university convocations and traditional dance presentations. Other items made from *songket* include cushions, handbags, table cloths, jewellery boxes, women's slippers as well as souvenir items. An interesting example of the use of *songket* is for decorative panels including those with verses from the Holy Quran.

Surau

A *surau* is a space or building used for Muslim prayers. It is generally much smaller than a mosque (*masjid*), hence the different name. As a general rule, large congregational prayer-assemblies, such as those for midday prayers on Friday or the major festivals (*Hari Raya*) are not held in *surau*, while congregational prayers involving smaller numbers for the five daily compulsory prayers commonly are. A *surau* does not have a permanent prayer leader (*imam*) as does a mosque. It also does not have a pulpit (*mimbar*). Other services such as classes for the teaching of Islam or the Holy Quran are available at many *surau*. Funeral (*janazah*) prayers and wedding ceremonies may also take place in them.

View of a *surau* in the outskirts of Kuching, Sarawak, Malaysia.
(Photo by Ghulam-Sarwar Yousof)

Syair

Syair is a form of traditional Malay poetry made up of four-line stanzas or quatrains. The word *syair* is derived from the Arabic word *shai'r*, a term that covers all genres of Arabic/Islamic poetry. However, the Malay form which goes by the name *syair* is somewhat different and not modelled on Arabic poetry or on any of the genres of Arab-Persian poetry. The *syair* can be a metrical romance, a narrative poem, a didactic poem or one used to convey ideas on religion or philosophy. It could even be one dealing with an historical event. The earliest known record of *syair* comes from the work of Hamzah Fansuri, a famous Indonesian poet of the 17th century. In contrast to *pantun*, the *syair* conveys a continuous idea from one stanza to the next, maintaining a unity of theme throughout, and each stanza is rhymed a-a-a-a-a. The best known examples from Malay literature are *Syair Bidasari*, *Syair Ken Tambuhan* and *Syair Panji Semirang*.

T

Tanah Melayu

The name *Tanah Melayu* (literally meaning Land of the Malays) is both interesting and confusing. It is evident that until the 19th century, the peninsula which extends from the Isthmus of Kra to Johor Bahru did not have a name. Loosely, part of it was known as Malacca until about 1800. There was no entity, political or otherwise, known as *Tanah Melayu* and when it came into use, it was not an indigenous one; the idea of calling it "Malay Peninsula" came from the British. This has caused many into mistakenly thinking that the Malays had their origins in the peninsula, and that it was a single political entity.

With the founding of Georgetown in Penang in 1786, the English seem to have generally adopted the usage of the term Malaya and in following decades, particularly after the 1824 Treaty, they began to see the whole of the peninsula with its autonomous sultanates as a coherent unit. However, at no time until the establishment of the Federated Malay States (*Persekutuan Tanah Melayu*) was *Tanah Melayu* officially used either as part or whole of the peninsula.

Tarik Selampit

Tarik selampit is a form of solo theatre active principally in the state of Kelantan on the east coast of the Malay Peninsula and in the Patani region of southern Thailand. Traditionally performed by blind singers, *tarik selampit* involves chanting, speaking and the assumption of various roles by a single performer, known as *tok selampit*, who accompanies himself on a three-stringed spiked fiddle (*rebab*). There is little actual movement of the artist during performances. Performances commence with a simple theatre opening (*buka panggung*) ceremony, offerings, some money (*wang pengkeras*), the burning of incense and invocations addressed to the human as well as spirit audience. The dramatic repertoire of *tarik selampit* consists of folk romances, most of which continue to exist in the oral tradition, although some attempt has been made to get them recorded and published.

Artist impression of a *tarik selampit* performer in Malaysia.
(Sketch by Fiona Wong)

Tekat

Tekat or *tekatan* is a form of embroidery with gold and silver thread, usually done on a base of velvet in several variant styles, depending upon whether the embroidery is flat or embossed. *Tekat* is historically connected with embroidery of Indian and Chinese courts from where it seems to have been transmitted to the Malay kingdoms from the time of the Melaka Sultanate (1400-1511). Some connections are also seen with the Middle East. Although *tekat* is known to have been active in several states, this art form is currently associated principally with Perak and Pahang. The royal town of Kuala Kangsar is a recognized centre for *tekat*.

This art was initially practiced at the courts where gold thread was used to achieve the embroidery as a means of decorating and the objects created for ceremonial as well as decorative use. *Tekat* may, for instance, following this tradition, still be seen on royal attire. Eventually, the use of *tekat* found its way into the life of the common man, with a range of objects created in *tekat* style to be used during weddings serving to decorate the bridal dais (*pelamin*) for the *bersanding* ceremony as well as the matrimonial bed. Beyond that, the art of *tekat* finds a place in the decoration of a range of items, including betel leaf (*sirih*) or jewellery boxes, fans (*kipas*), women's sandals, cushion covers as well as framed pieces to decorate walls.

Tekat embroidery mat. (Photo by Ghulam-Sarwar Yousof)

Tidakapathy

Sometimes shortened to *tak apa* or *tak pa*, the two words *tidak* and *apa* literally mean "there is nothing", but the actual sense is better suggested by "it does not matter" or "never mind", the attitude of not worrying or not caring, termed by some in popular parlance through the use of a neologism *tidakapathy*, composed of *tidak+apa+*pathy. When things go wrong (not very wrong, however), the general reaction among the Malays is one of *tidak apa*. In some ways, this may reflect their background as a people who traditionally did not worry too much, did not suffer stress or did not care too much for anything, their ability to live simply with little since Nature provided much of what was needed. It may even suggest a forgiving nature, that of willing to give and take or compromise (*tolak ansur*). Finally, it may suggest an attitude of care-less-ness, of not being bothered, these days expressed in new ways, including what has come to be known as the *lepak* syndrome.

Changing circumstances and modernisation have naturally altered some of these qualities as Malays have become more aggressively demanding. Even then, basically, *tidakapathy* still persists, often with disastrous results such as laziness, inefficiency or loss of productivity.

Tolak Bala

Tolak bala is a complex of ritual activities aimed at avoiding something evil or troublesome which may come through the involvement of a spirit (*hantu* or *jembalang*) as well as some misfortune (*bala*) happening to a person or the community. In the case of an individual, *tolakbala* means to prevent or control malice through means such as wearing of charms and amulets (*azimat* or *tangkal*) or carrying them on the person. Certain times (*waktu, ketika*) are considered unsuitable for particular activities and thus it becomes necessary to avoid them. Particular activities can also be done to avoid *bala*. One should, for instance, save unfinished food rather than throw it away; give a salutation (*salam*) before urinating at certain places in the environment including public pathways; make a food offering (*kenduri*) when there is a natural calamity or some form of accident from which one emerges unscathed. The practice of *tolak bala*, in such situations, is in fact an act of thanksgiving. It indicates a fusion of pre-Islamic and Islamic ideas and practices. In keeping with traditional beliefs, the practice of *tolak bala* became institutionalized through rituals such as the paying of homage to sea spirits in the *puja pantai* ritual. Such rites generally fuse pre-Islamic beliefs and those which came with Islam, including verses from the Holy Quran, supplications (*doa*) as well as food offerings (*sajian*) to resident spirits (*penunggu*) at certain localities. Recent years, however, have seen a gradual abandonment of some, but not all, of these practices.

Toyol

A *toyol* or *tuyul* is a little child spirit acquired from an aborted foetus by means of black magic. It is believed to look like a naked baby, with a big head, small hands, clouded eyes and usually greenish skin. It has to be treated by a child with appropriate food offerings. Bound to a *bomoh*, it is used mainly to steal things from other people.

U

Ulik mayang

Ulik mayang is a traditional trance dance from the state of Terengganu on the east coast of Peninsular Malaysia. It is performed to invoke or appease the spirits of the sea and is always accompanied by a unique, haunting song also called *ulik mayang*. Dancers also make use of *mayang*, the frond of the coconut palm. A traditional orchestra comprising drums, gong, violin and accordion accompanies the dance. An interesting origin story links this genre with a fisherman in a romantic situation, the abduction of his soul, efforts to heal him by shaman, as well as a battle between the shaman and six sea-princesses. The matter is finally settled by the intercession of the seventh sea-princess, who significantly declares that those whose origins lie in the sea should return to the sea and those from the land return to the land. The *bomoh* and his companions make offerings of coloured rice to the spirits of the sea. Like several other traditional Malay performing arts, *ulik mayang* has suffered decline in recent decades due to the influence of orthodox Islam.

Urut

Urut or *urut kampung*, village massage, is a native Malay massage technique which has much in common with massage from Indonesia, and in the urban centres of the country Javanese practitioners may be encountered.

In *urut kampung*, the male or female masseur (*tukang urut*) clasps the muscles, usually of the back, shoulder or limb, tightly and then draws the hand along with great pressure. This form of massage is generally done using specially prepared herbal oils or creams. It is intended to serve various purposes, including easing pain or headache, reducing stress and bringing about relaxation of the body or general wellbeing.

Tukang urut claims for *urut kampung* include all manner of cures including the bringing down of high blood pressure, curing diabetes, removing kidney stones. Special techniques may also be used by the *tukang urut* to induce abortion in cases of early pregnancy or assist in post-partum recovery or, in the case of men, enhance sexual potency. Herbal pills, powders or other native concoctions may be included as part of the cure. Traditional *tukang urut* at times use a combination of massage and Islamic supplications.

In spite of the ready availability of modern medicine, there seems to be an increasing demand for *tukang urut kampung*, just like that for the traditional healer (*bomoh*), even in the country's urban centres, with practitioners resorting to advertising in Malay language tabloids or popular magazines. It is not uncommon for such practitioners of massage to combine Malay techniques with those used in Thai or Chinese massage, particularly foot reflexology.

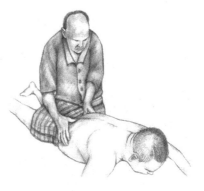

Artist iimpression of a traditional Malay *urut*. (Sketch by Fiona Wong)

W

Wau

Two terms are used in Malaysia to refer to the kite: *layang-layang* for the basic kites and *wau* for the much larger and more elaborate ones. While kite-making and -flying may be encountered almost everywhere in the country, the most elaborate and striking kites are seen principally in the Kelantan and Terengganu. Kites are made of a variety of materials, depending upon their final use as items for decoration or for flying. Among the best known are *wau bulan* (moon kite), *wau burung* (bird kite), *wau katak* (frog kite), *wau daun* (leaf kite), *wau helang* (eagle kite), *wau kucing* (cat kite) and *wau merak* (peacock kite). Apart from those already mentioned, it is not unusual to find innovative or creative designs, including kites taking the human form.

The process of making a kite is complicated and elaborate. The whole process can take up to two weeks for a particularly elaborate kite. It begins with the preparation of the kite-frame (*rangka*), which is made of thin jointed sections of bamboo, and checked for its balance. The various section of the frame and put together and tied with thread. Basically, the frame of the kite consists of several sections: the head (*kepala*), the wings (*sayap*), the tail (*ekor*) or tail fin (*tanduk*), with a spine or midrib (*tulang belakang*) running through and joining the wings and the tail.

While normally kite-making is regarded with some importance since it incorporates so many different arts, as in many countries, kite-flying in Malaysia serves as a source of entertainment as well as serving to celebrate a good harvest. Beyond that, in Kelantan particularly, kite-flying is also a serious sport demanding great skill. Contests are usually held after the harvest season.

The function of driving away evil spirits through the use of kites, however, is not altogether absent in Kelantan when the kites have risen to the maximum height and are stable. This purpose is served by the attachment of a *busul* that makes a humming sound. This is a piece of split leaf fibre (*daun busar*) shaped like a violinist's bow. Held under tension between the ends, it is fixed transversely to the back of the kite and emits a loud low-pitched note or harmony of notes when the wind blows across it.

Principally, however, the best-designed and executed kites are appreciated for their beauty based upon the intricacy of design and the craftsmanship involved. With this in mind, kites are also made of batik material or silk instead of paper, these often being much smaller than kites intended for competitions.

Artist impression of a moon kite (*wau bulan*),
a popular type of kite in Malaysia.
(Sketch by Fiona Wong)

Wayang

The word *wayang*, which may be translated as performance or show, is a generic word used for any kind of performance. In Bahasa Melayu or Bahasa Indonesia, it frequently appears in a combination with *kulit* (skin or leather), thus referring to the shadow play (*wayang kulit*), of which many forms are active in Indonesia while Malaysia has three. There are many other uses for this word in Indonesia for various genres of theatre, such as *wayang golek*, *wayang orang* and so on which are not active in Malaysia. When it comes to the human theatre forms in Malaysia, the word *wayang* is also used to refer to the operatic form known as *bangsawan*, thus it is known as *wayang bangsawan*, and Chinese opera is known as *wayang Cina*. Finally, in the modern context, this term also is used in the form of *wayang gambar* to refer to the film. In both bangsawan and Chinese opera, the word *wayang* combined with *anak* (*anak wayang*) refers to the actors or performers rather than to the genre.

A rather unusual and modern usage, though technically incorrect, the term appears in Malaysian Parliamentary debates to refer to activity or behaviour considered frivolous, not serious or even untrue. Such activity is referred to as performing theatre (*main wayang*) or even as *wayang kulit*, *bangsawan* or *sandiwara*, various kinds of theatre discussed in separate entries. This, of course, shows ignorance of the seriousness of theatre amongst Parliamentarians.

Wayang Kulit Kelantan

The *wayang kulit* (shadow play) is a theatre in which two-dimensional puppets made from animal skin are used to cast shadows upon a white muslin screen by means of a light source, traditionally an oil lamp, but these days an electric bulb. In Malaysia, three types of shadow play have been active in recent years. *Wayang kulit purwa, wayang kulit gedek* and *wayang kulit Siam*, also known as *wayang kulit Kelantan*. Active in Kelantan as well as northern Terengganu, this is the most important of the three. It makes use of a repertoire of stories based upon a local version of the Indian epic, Ramayana, known as *Hikayat Maharaja Wana*, as well as branch stories of this epic invented by the puppeteers themselves.

A *wayang kulit Kelantan* set consists of about 60 figures made of cow skin and ranging in height from about six to nine inches to over two feet. The principal ones represent Ramayana characters while secondary characters include ogres, clowns and servants. Both in physical appearance and details of design, they conform to certain Malay aesthetic principles while at the same time accommodating Hindu, Thai and Javanese concepts. Apart from human and ogre figures, the most important figure in a *wayang kulit Kelantan* set is a tree or leaf image, known as *pohon beringin*, which is used to both open and close performances.

The central figure in any *wayang kulit* performance is the master puppeteer (*dalang* or *tok dalang*). Apart from manipulating the puppets, he provides voices to all his characters and develops the plot through dialogue, narration, commentary and the use of songs. In addition, he functions as the conductor of the *wayang* orchestra and as a ritual specialist (*bomoh*).

Music for a *wayang kulit Kelantan* performance is provided by an orchestra consisting of a pair of drums (*gendang*), a pair of goblet-shaped drums (*gedumbak*), a pair of standing drums (*gedug*) beaten with sticks, a pair of bronze gongs, a pair of small gongs (*canang*) placed in a wooden rack, a pair of cymbals (*kesi*) and a double-reed oboe (*serunai*). Seven or eight musicians are usually required to play music during a performance.

Wayang kulit Kelantan performances take place in a temporary theatre (*panggung*) generally made of wood and thatched palm leaf (*attap*) and raised between three to four feet above the ground. The completely open front side of the theatre is concealed by means of a screen (*kelir*) stretched tight across.

During a performance, the figures are planted on two banana stems (*batang pisang*) placed at the bottom of the screen inside the *panggung*. Suspended from the top and positioned roughly at screen-centre is an oil lamp or electric bulb which causes shadows of the puppets to fall on the *kelir*. Spectators sit on the grass or on benches.

Performances begin at about 9:00 p.m. after the final (*isya*) prayer with a theatre opening ritual (*upacara buka panggung*) and a section done by an apprentice puppeteer (*dalang muda*), who takes his position at the *panggung* front, roughly at the same position as the lamp and is thus able to use it to cast shadows of his figures. During this prelude, the principal characters of the Ramayana are introduced and Rama, the hero, is glorified. Following this, a regular puppeteer performs a selected episode. Normal performances last from a few minutes to several hours, depending upon the situation; each performance ends with a simple theatre closing (*tutup panggung*) ceremony.

Opening scene from the *wayang kulit* shadow play in Kelantan, Malaysia.
(Photo by Ghulam-Sarwar Yousof)

Selected References

Braginsky, Vladimir. *The Heritage of Traditional Malay Literature.* Singapore: Institute of Southeast Asian Studies, 2004.

Dewan Bahasa dan Pustaka. *Ensiklopedia Sejarah dan Kebudayaan Melayu.* Kuala Lumpur: Dewan Bahasa dan Pustaka, 1995.

Ghulam-Sarwar Yousof. *Dictionary of Traditional Southeast Asian Theatre.* Singapore: Oxford University Press, 1994.

Sheppard, Mubin. *Taman Indera: A Royal Pleasure Ground.* Kuala Lumpur: Oxford, 1972.

Skeat, Walter William. *Malay Magic.* New York: Benjamin Blom, 1972.

Wilkinson, R. J. *A Malay-English Dictionary.* London: MacMillan & Co Ltd, 1957.

PROFESSOR DATO' DR. GHULAM-SARWAR YOUSOF

Prof. Dato' Dr. Ghulam-Sarwar Yousof graduated in English from the University of Malaya (1964), and did a Doctorate in Asian Theatre at the University of Hawaii (1976). He is one of Malaysia's most distinguished scholars of performing arts and one of the world's leading specialists of traditional Southeast Asian theatre.

He was responsible for setting up Malaysia's first Performing Arts programme at the Science University of Malaysia (USM) in Penang in 1970. Prof. Ghulam-Sarwar Yousof served at that university as lecturer and Associate Professor. He joined the Cultural Centre, University of Malaya (UM) as Professor in 2002 to 2009. He also served as a Senior Academic Fellow at the Department of English Language and Literature, International Islamic University Malaysia, from 2009 to 2014. At the same time, he continued to serve in University of Malaya as an Expert.

Currently, he is an Adjunct Professor at the Cultural Centre, University of Malaya, Kuala Lumpur. He is also Director of The Asian Cultural Heritage Centre Berhad, a private research initiative set up by him to promote research in traditional Asian cultures.

Apart from traditional Asian theatre, his major interests include Asian literatures, folklore studies, as well as South- and Southeast Asian cultures, comparative religion, mythology and, Sufism. In ethnographic and folklore studies he has explored Malay-Indonesian mythology and folk literature, Malay concepts of the soul (*semangat*), and *angin* as well as their place in healing processes involving traditional theatre. He is also involved in a research project on Malay-Indonesian aesthetics.

As a creative writer, he has published poetry, drama as well as short stories. He has also done a translation of Kalidasa's Sanskrit play *Shakuntala* as well as translations of Urdu poetry into English. Among other things, he is currently working on a volume of ghazal translations into English as well as an anthology of Islamic Literature.

Dato' Ghulam-Sarwar Yousof's most outstanding contribution to academia is in traditional Southeast Asian Theatre. In this area he has carved a unique niche for himself, with meticulous field work and research in some previously unexplored genres, resulting in the most important existing publication on the subject, his *Dictionary of Traditional Southeast Asian Theatre* (Oxford, 1994). His vast collection of fieldwork materials and documentation is currently held by the Asian Cultural Heritage Centre Berhad.

Dato' Ghulam-Sarwar Yousof has held visiting positions as a professor at several universities, has lectured in many countries in both Asia and Europe on a broad spectrum of culture-related subjects and on altogether unclassifiable disciplines alike to absolute novices and specialized audiences. He has also given readings of his poetry and short stories as well as organized major poetry events in Kuala Lumpur and Penang in conjunction with UNESCO World Poetry Day. He has been, over the decades, involved in various capacities in numerous cultural organizations, national and international, including the Asia-Europe Foundation as Malaysia's official representative and member of the foundation's Board of Governors.

Academic Awards

1. East-West Centre Grant for a Doctoral Programme at the Department of Drama and Theatre, University of Hawaii, Honolulu, USA. *September 1972 to September 1976.*
2. Universiti Sains Malaysia Academic Staff Training Scheme (ASTS) Fellowship for a Doctoral Programme at the Department of Drama and Theatre, University of Hawaii, Honolulu, USA. *September 1972 to September 1977.*
3. Universiti Sains Malaysia, Penang, Research Grants for Research, Field Work and Documentation of Traditional Malay Theatre Genres. *1978 to 1994.*
4. Institute of Southeast Asian Studies, Singapore, Research Grant. *June 1983-June 1984.*
5. Southeast Asian Studies Programme (SEASP), Institute of Southeast Asian Studies, Singapore, Teaching and Research Exchange Fellowships Award. *June 1983 to March 1984.*
6. Southeast Asian Studies Programme (SEASP), Institute of Southeast Asian Studies, Singapore, Cross-Cultural Research and Writing Award. *June 1983 to March 1984.*

Awards of Recognition

1. Tokoh Maal-Hijrah (Persatuan Melayu Pulau Pinang), 2001.
2. International Award for Outstanding Contribution for Humanity, Peace, Culture and Education (Forum for Culture and Human Development, Bangladesh), 2001.
3. Dove Award for Excellence in Poetry awarded (Poetry Day Australia), 2001.
4. Darjah Setia Pangkuan Negeri (DSPN), which carries the title of Dato' awarded by the Tuan Yang Terutama Yang DiPertua Negeri Pulau Pinang (Governor of Penang), 2008.
5. Boh Cameronian Lifetime Achievement Award (Kakiseni Malaysia), 2008.

Books

1. **Ceremonial and Decorative Crafts of Penang**. Penang: State Museum, 1986.
2. **Bibliography of Traditional Theatre in Southeast Asia**. Singapore: Institute of Southeast Asian Studies, 1991.
3. **Panggung Semar: Aspects of Traditional Malay Theatre**. Kuala Lumpur: Tempo Publishing (M) Sdn. Bhd., 1992.
4. **Dictionary of Traditional Southeast Asian Theatre**. Kuala Lumpur: Oxford University Press, 1994.
5. **Angin Wayang: Biography of a Master Puppeteer**. Kuala Lumpur: Ministry of Culture, Arts and Tourism, 1997.
6. **Angin Wayang: Biografi Seorang Dalang yang Unggul**. Kuala Lumpur: Ministry of Culture, Arts and Tourism, 1997.
7. **The Malay Shadow Play: An Introduction**. Penang: the Asian Centre, 1997.
8. **Reflections on Asian-European Epics**. Editor: Ghulam-Sarwar Yousof. Singapore: Editions Didier Millet, Archipelago Press, 2004.
9. **Panggung Inu: Aspects of Traditional Malay Theatre**. Singapore: National University of Singapore Cultural Centre, 2004.
10. **Encyclopedia of Malaysia. Vol 8, Performing Arts**. Editor: Ghulam-Sarwar Yousof. Singapore: Archipelago Press. Editions Didier Millet, 2004.
11. **Heritage of ASEAN Puppetry**. Jakarta: SENA WANGI. 2013.
12. Nakayama, Machiko. **500 Years of Ikebana**. Editor: Ghulam-Sarwar Yousof. Kuala Lumpur: The Asian Cultural Heritage Centre Bhd, 2013.
13. **Selected Papers on Traditional Malay Theatre.** (Tokoh Melayu Series). Kuala Lumpur, 2014.
14. **Issues in Traditional Malaysian Culture.** Singapore: Trafford Publishing, 2013, Reissued by Partridge, Singapore, 2014.
15. **Puppetry for All Times: Papers Presented at Bali Puppetry Seminar 2013.** Editor: Ghulam-Sarwar Yousof. Singapore: Partridge, 2014.

Monographs

1. *Muslim Festivals: Essence and Observance.* Islamic Information Centre, Malayan Pakistani League, Penang, 1989.
2. *Traditional Theatre in Southeast Asia: An Introduction.* Penang: Pusat Seni, Universiti Sains Malaysia, 1993. Monographs on Southeast Asian Cultures series.
3. *Mak Yong Theatre of Kelantan, Malaysia: An Introduction.* Kuala Lumpur: The Asian Cultural Heritage Centre Berhad, 2011.

Literary Publications

1. Ghulam-Sarwar Yousof. *Perfumed Memories.* Singapore: Graham Brash Pte Ltd., 1982. (Collection of Poems)
2. Ghulam-Sarwar Yousof. *Halfway Road, Penang. Penang.* Teks Publishing Company, (1982). Reprinted by The Asian Cultural Heritage Centre, Penang, 2002. (Drama text)
3. Ghulam-Sarwar Yousof. *Mirror of a Hundred Hues: A Miscellany.* Penang: The Asian Cultural Heritage Centre, 2001.
4. Ghulam-Sarwar Yousof. *Songs for Shooting Stars: Mystical Verse.* Pittsburgh, PA15222, USA: Lauriat Press, 2011. (Selected Poems)
5. Ghulam-Sarwar Yousof. *Transient Moments.* Kuala Lumpur: The Asian Cultural Heritage Centre, 2012. (Selected Poems)
6. Ghulam-Sarwar Yousof. (Editor) *The Asian Centre Anthology of Malaysian Poetry in English.* Singapore: Partridge, 2014.
7. Ghulam-Sarwar Yousof. *The Trial of Hang Tuah the Great: A Play in Nine Scenes.* Singapore" Partridge, 2014.
8. Ghulam-Sarwar Yousof. *Tok Dalang and Stories of Other Malaysians.* Singapore: Partridge, 2014.
9. Ghulam-Sarwar Yousof. *Suvarna-Padma, The Golden Lotus.* Singapore: Partridge, 2015.
10. Ghulam-Sarwar Yousof. *Sacred Rain.* Singapore: Partridge, 2015.

Printed in the United States
By Bookmasters